The METAPHYSICIAN
Within

What people are saying about
The MetaPhysician Within

"This book is phenomenal and powerful... concise and completely accurate ... and gently with such compassion speaks to you as if the author was sitting with you guiding and helping you to heal. So much depth lies in this book one is drawn to re-read it over and over again and share it with everyone."

– Michelle, South Africa

"The quality of the information, healing, creativity and love shared is amazing! Lisa gives us the tools to explore, heal ourselves and create a healing practice as we meet the "The Metaphysician Within". - I highly recommend this book."

– Andrea, California

"More than a diagnostic tool and a means for gaining new understanding about one's body, The MetaPhysican Within *represents a new and marvelous way of seeing the metaphysical in the physical. This way of seeing and being comes through from a heart anchored firmly in love and a deeply intuitive mind."*

– Jim, Maryland

"After reading Lisa's metaphysical essays I was stunned by the psycho-spiritual significance of the information! I have Crohn's disease and use her essays for my own healing."

– Karen, New York City

"The MetaPhysician Within is amazing... this book is a treasure! Thank you very much for sending it into the world. The more I read, the more I understand that each metaphysical essay has something to offer anyone...I read it daily!"

– El, The Netherlands

"This book is "spiritual medicine"... I keep it handy on my iPhone and use it to help myself and others all the time!"

– Ewelina, Poland

"The MetaPhysician Within is truly inspiring. I'm working to let go of so many things and finding the ability to heal my body and soul and share the God inspired love within me. Thank you for sharing your insights with the world!"

– Stephanie, Ohio

"My Life has changed dramatically because of the amazing metaphysical insights and healing energy Lisa offers."

– Carla, Arizona

"I was mesmerized... this book sheds light on the anatomy of illnesses that plagued people near and dear to me! I recommend this book to anyone struggling to understand the emotional anatomy of illness. Lisa radiates warmth that is restorative... her book is an extension of her boundless energy and healing."

- Jill, New Jersey

Dear
Dear Marion
You are so amazing
and I would
Love to
connect
with you
more often

Loving Love
Jeff Bloch
4-27-14

LISA A. BLACKMAN PUBLISHING
Fairfield, CT 06824
www.lisablackman.org

ISBN: 978-0-9841802-6-4
LCCN 2010915454
Copyright © 2012 Lisa A. Blackman
© 2012 Photographic Images by Lisa A. Blackman

Medical Disclaimer

Information contained in this book is intended to generate understanding and overall well-being. The author and publisher accept no responsibility for the application of any of the information provided herein. If you have any health concerns please seek medical assistance.

The
METAPHYSICIAN
Within
A Reference for Healing

Lisa A. Blackman

LISA A. BLACKMAN PUBLISHING
Fairfield, CT 06824
www.lisablackman.org

"Every place where there is an absence of Love is a condition that needs mending."

- Lisa A. Blackman

DEDICATION

I dedicate this book to the evolution of humankind in the hopes of bringing healing, teaching, and unconditional love to this planet and beyond.

With God's blessing,

To The MetaPhysician Within you, I give to you myself,

Lisa

The MetaPhysician
Within

CONTENTS

The MetaPhysician Within

INTRODUCTION

Awaken The MetaPhysician Within and Heal Yourself

All of us has, or has had, some condition of the mind or body, some debilitating, painful or frustrating ailment that can frighten us, confuse us, and bring our spirits down, negatively affecting our lives, as well as the lives of others. Our conditions may range from grief to cancer to alcoholism to bipolar disorder to back issues to obesity to heart problems to depression. The list is endless. To deal with these maladies, we see doctors and/or therapists, we take medications, we read up on our conditions on the internet, we talk to others who suffer the same conditions and sometimes to just about anyone who will listen to us.

Even those of us who call upon prayer, meditation, alternative healers, spiritual teachers, life coaches, yoga, fitness programs, and healthy diets sometimes find ourselves prone to short-term or chronic conditions. It seems that no matter how hard we try, we often feel that something is missing, some elusive part of the movement toward healing and wholeness that we just naturally strive for with every breath that we take. We can become unnecessarily desperate and lost with our conditions, and at times mysterious, nearly mystical discomfort or pain that can come and go and for some even remain constant. Eventually, we are given a diagnosis of something such as fibromyalgia and we remain in pain. Many people suffer for years before finding relief and/or meaning of any kind and often end up accepting pain that they need not accept and learn to live with it. We are told or tell ourselves to ignore our symptoms and they will go away, which is like saying ignore your soul and it will disappear. Our souls are very powerful and will always find a way to be heard so that our spiritual mark - our destiny - is not missed or left to fate.

We now have the ability to more easily transform our pain into passion and positive action as there is an enormous awakening of the Spirit pulsating throughout the world today. There are, however, still too many people suffering. Whether it is physical, emotional, mental, and/or spiritual pain, it works together as one body and we must understand its voice - this language of the soul. There is a divine purpose to all of our pain - no one is suffering alone or in vain.

If you sense that there is something more to dealing with your own pain or challenging condition, or an ailment that a loved one or someone in your care is suffering with, you are right. I believe that the missing ingredient is a deeper understanding of why an illness or symptom of the mind, body, and soul exists. Your body's symptoms and emotions are trying to tell you something - something vitally important that must be honored. Your conditions are the secret language of your soul and when you learn to decode that language you will reveal your own personal story, the story that is the key to healing yourself spiritually.

It is crucial to our souls that they be *read,* which means to be seen - purely seen - so we create symptoms, or one condition after the next, all metaphysically designed to encourage us to delve more deeply within, leading us in the direction of the higher self while simultaneously dissolving the ego. The ego is the shadow side of human beings formed by the *scars of fear* we carry caused by our wounding. We are constantly given opportunities to individuate into the Godself as we recuperate from the conditions of our lives, whether physical, mental, emotional, financial, relational, or a combination of these and/or others. The language of our spirit lies in our bodies and minds.

There is no need to have a heart attack, manifest a fibroid tumor, have unexplained muscular or pelvic pain, live with headaches, suffer with irritable bowel syndrome, etc., in order to mature spiritually, remove our blocks, and make necessary changes in our lives while we solidify and fully make conscious connection with the Divine. Intuitive Healing, Sacred Cosmic Psychology, and Medical Intuition are rapidly growing fields and a vital part of our well-being that must now be considered along with any and all others. The correct language needs to be spoken and taught and we must now homeschool ourselves about *ourselves* while working along with our healthcare providers as well as our loved ones in order to accelerate the healing of everyone. Human beings have always applied their own intuition to some degree while healing themselves and others. However, it is important to remember and be aware that our perceptions are clouded by our wounding. Illness, symptoms, and any life situation or condition we are faced with *is* that wounding waiting to be revealed so it can be healed as we simultaneously learn to love ourselves and others more unconditionally. In learning how to love we learn to see everything and everyone more clearly, including our conditions and their highest meanings, mission, and purpose. We learn how to see with the eyes we were born with - those of the Divine.

The root cause of all pain is the absence of love, so anyplace where there *is* an absence of love *is* a condition that needs mending. God is Spirit purified; therefore, spiritual healing is the most important part of how we heal, how we begin to purify our souls. Doing so means taking, what for many of you may be a new and exciting step while others may find the path natural and familiar, an extension of your own spiritual exploration and work. It means remembering, awakening, and activating The MetaPhysician Within. We are each in a state of remembrance - remembering who we *really* are and why we are here – whether fully conscious of this or not. The MetaPhysician Within is the one who honors, listens to, and understands the language of the soul that uses the body and mind as its voice. It is your higher self - Godself

- your most holy and pure self. The MetaPhysician Within is the one who is aware at every and any moment what it is that you need and desire most in order to live a balanced and healthy life full of love, joy, youthfulness, creativity, purpose, ecstatic moments, and Spirit. In other words, all negativity in our life is replaced with full positivity. All things become holy and sacred to the touch of our spirit as one.

The essays presented in this book are from my collection of intuited healing readings, which some call medical intuition, and are placed in alphabetical order. They will guide you in activating this MetaPhysician Within and support you in practicing this in your everyday life. They will help you wherever you may be in your life and spiritual journey, and whatever condition of the body, mind, or spirit you may currently be struggling with or have suffered at any time in the past without fully understanding what happened, what it meant, and how it could help you heal and transform your life. These 36 metaphysical essays on common or chronic conditions, whether or not they have any known cure, can empower you to take charge and heal yourself by learning what is emotionally, spiritually, and metaphysically causing your conditions and symptoms of mind and body.

My hope is that *The MetaPhysician Within* can be a bible of love and healing for you. I invite you to call upon it as a reference book for any condition of the body and mind. These insights are like sacred prescriptions, divinely designed to be used on a regular basis as a meditation, prayer, healing tool, and/or study guide. They can serve as a strong and sturdy bridge into the unseen world of Spirit, encouraging and greatly supporting your journey to wholeness and health of mind, body, and spirit.

You may feel, as you read from the essays, that you are receiving an intuitive reading. Your vibration will rise and your intuition will open as well as your heart and mind as you discover your truth and divinity while you travel to the places you need to go in the moment. You will naturally develop increased unconditional love and compassion for yourself and others, as you will be reading about their conditions, too. You will be able to more easily forgive current hurts and those from long ago. You will learn why you attract who and what you do in your life and what has been holding you back. You will find out how to make positive changes in your life. You will understand why you are frustrated, angry, unforgiven and unforgiving, tired all the time, overeating, drinking, feeling anxious, fearful, resentful, and/or out of touch or alignment anywhere in body, mind and spirit. Your connection to the Divine will be more cherished and evolved after reading the book as well as refreshed and solidified.

There is a shadow side of illness that mirrors our own shadow and it is spiritually and neutrally revealed in *The MetaPhysician Within*. Revealing the shadow is crucial for our evolution as a whole. It is important when dealing with the shadow that it is embraced rather than hidden or feared because our greatest light is hiding beneath it and in order to access our light we must meet this shadow in ourselves and others. It is my prayer and greatest hope that *The MetaPhysician Within* brings the greatest light to the collective shadow of the world.

The Divine Revelations contained within these essays have been designed and presented to generate understanding and the wisdom of the true voice of the soul and to accelerate your spiritual remembrance, awakening, and healing process. It is not designed to point fingers, judge, or blame anyone, or to disengage you with your healthcare providers. It will aid you in seeing more clearly the reality and vulnerability of the unseen child within yourself and others who is fully ready for and needs love and care on a more unconditional and deeper level, a more real level. When our shadow side is revealed we are then free to heal ourselves further and empower others to heal themselves, too. We become more real, which means to be more of the Divine Reality that we really are. This book offers a sacred medical psychology utilizing intuitional spiritual guidance as its tool of excavation of the meaning and sublime reasoning of illness, allowing you to make better decisions and choices in your life, which ultimately affects the lives of all as one.

In reading the essay of one condition that has troubled you or someone you love and/or care for, you are likely to quickly *see* yourself or them and begin to feel a sense of calmness as fear dissipates and the higher self is activated. Reducing or eliminating fear is crucial because fear can create as well as accelerate symptoms and illness and dramatically slow down the healing process. You may discover that the condition that is causing or has caused you pain has not ruined your life or the life of someone close to you, but rather has been a holy event doing the divine work to save your life by offering opportunity to catapult you into a more purposeful, exciting, and love-filled creative life. To know this truth and work with it can help you turn all of your pain into passion and radical divine action of the highest formulation.

I began writing these essays over 15 years ago for clients, friends, family, and even for myself. For nearly 20 years I have been a practicing spiritual healer, providing intuitive consultations for individuals, couples, families, and groups of all ages and walks of life. The essays developed as a natural progression, expansion, and exploration of my work. I remember one early experience that helped to lay the foundation for these writings. A friend's daughter-in-law, a mother with young sons just like myself at the time, had been diagnosed with multiple sclerosis. I felt so much compassion, and although I had never met her, I believed I could help her and her family. I desired to formulate a diagnosis for her using my intuition, so I prayed, "Dear God, where does the condition of MS come from and how can Allison heal herself". (Please do not be distracted by my choice of using the name God in the essays and by all means replace it with whatever term you are comfortable with using for the Divine.)

I had prayed this way many times before journaling or doing an intuitive reading for myself while discovering and healing my own spirit, as well as working as a spiritual guide and mentor for others and still work this way today. I had discovered automatic writing or channeling to be the most efficient way for me to serve the most people at the same time while being the least disruptive and most supportive of my family life. I prayed to receive information effortlessly and without edit and that is exactly what occurred every time. I would ask God, or what sometimes I referred to as *Spirit Life,* for insight on specific topics I was interested in such as the world of Spirit, enlightenment, and the overall evolution of the world and its people. I quickly filled journals and notebooks and was literally consumed with my newfound calling and exuberance of Spirit that demanded to be shared.

It wasn't until around my time with Allison and my writing on MS, however, that I thought seriously to do a reading for specific conditions of the body or mind. I simply began writing down what I was hearing clairvoyantly and just knowing clairsentiently about the condition of MS. My goal was to help Allison gain clarity, composure, and healing so that she could focus on what she could do to take responsibility and heal herself. After sharing my writing with her I was so gratified to hear that it helped her tremendously. I was excited, too, to have discovered a wonderful new way to help others on a more universal level as I had then realized that we are one in Spirit as well as in our conditions.

As I further reflected on this new experience I realized that the roots of my seeking spiritual answers for physical and mental conditions could be traced to my childhood. Growing up I was the only daughter and youngest of three children. My father was ill and suffered terribly, becoming crippled, blinded, and eventually bedridden by disease, which his doctors all agreed, at the time, was the worst case they had ever treated. He was diagnosed with ankylosing spondylitis, rheumatoid arthritis, and iritis. As early as three years old I was aware that something was not right and remember watching him become more ill with each passing year. By the time I was 12 years old, he had lost much of his strength and would soon lose his eyesight as well due to complications of the illness. He could no longer walk well or work and was forced to retire from a job he loved and was very good at. This was of course financially and emotionally difficult in many ways but also meant he would be at home with me each day after school. It was very hard as a child to watch my father suffer and not be able to help, especially for someone whom everyone regarded as very wise, charismatic, and inspiring. My parents hid as much as they could about my father's illness from my brothers and me out of protection and desire to provide us with the most natural and normal childhood they could. It is of no surprise, then, that I would grow up and become a "spiritual investigator" of mind and body suffering.

A year or two after my intuitive reading for Allison, she had sent me a letter and a news clipping of an article about her, with a photo of her and her children. She had been selected as Mother of the Year for the MS Foundation. She found true joy, purpose, and harmony in her own life while also becoming an inspiration to others. Although at the time the MS had not gone away completely, she certainly had healed her spirit. Rather than regarding her condition as a sentence of pain and misery, she used it as a catalyst to discover her Divine mission and purpose. She could now clearly see how MS had been a gift in disguise.

Another early essay emerged while I was in the waiting room of a doctor's office. I was growing impatient waiting for my friend Mary who believed she was having a heart attack. I had a strong sense she was experiencing anxiety and having a panic attack, so I asked God what anxiety really was, why we suffer with it, and how we can heal from it. Again, an insightful and very helpful message emerged. For the first time Mary was able to go into a crowded grocery store without experiencing anxiety and/or having a panic attack. She had used the prayer I gave to her: "*Dear God, please replace my fear with faith*" and two powerful affirmations: "*I am balanced, I am one with God*" and "*No fear lives here!*" She was able to finally get through parts of her life without the pain of panic, which many of us can relate to as ranging from mild to excruciating at times. That essay has proved quite handy for myself and many others who have or would have experienced some form of anxiety. Soon Mary was able to release her need for the medication prescribed for her condition. She understood clearly the Divine purpose anxiety especially plays in the way our spirits lead us into the light of the higher self.

Since those early experiences, I have written dozens of essays about a host of other conditions. Those who needed them just showed up in my life one by one or sometimes I would hear of someone who was suffering with something or I would have an intuitive hit to write about a specific condition. A friend, Donna, had called me in terrible pain while driving our children to a party. I told her I believed she had sciatica and read her that essay that I had previously written for someone else. By the time I finished reading it, the pain, which she had been suffering with for one month, had disappeared. Donna was able to integrate the healing insights given to release the pain she was carrying. I also sensed that hearing it read by me helped her to feel the energy and love she needed to comprehend and absorb the insights, while feeling safe enough to let go of the pain stored in her body.

Sometimes, of course, it takes reading an essay more than once to integrate its teachings. Everyone is different and has varying needs in the frequency of reading the essays. Keep in mind that each time an essay is read you will likely see something new and have an opening. Our souls are often designed to evolve a bit at a time because it can be difficult to integrate emotionally too much at once for the sake of the soul and those in connection with that soul. I firmly believe, however, that this work will speed things up considerably, but safely. Healing will be obvious, as you will feel confirmation, enlivenment, invigoration, expansion, lightness, more confidence, and spiritually connected. Also, when symptoms begin or get more intense is always a good time to read a specific essay or even choose one randomly from the book. There are universal spiritual truths and teachings woven throughout. When feeling disconnected to your spirit, anxious, angry, or fearful is also a very good time to read from *The MetaPhysician Within*. Keep in mind that any discomfort is often a silent scream for spiritual healing.

Spiritual growth is always being offered to us and something new to learn and be working on is most always available, as the Earth plane is a school we are guests upon and each of us have our unique curriculum, but we are learning the same lessons leading us to return to our core essence, love. That is part of what makes this work such an exciting self-discovery tool. At our deepest core we are the ones in charge and responsible for our own healing and enlightenment. The support we need in the physical world naturally shows up as we do our part and are ready to meet another one of the key players in our spiritual awakening and remembrance of our divinity, which coincides with our spiritual healing and soul's evolution. Those who are destined to come into our lives by what some call "Divine appointment" to play their roles just do, and eventually we evolve to a point where we really know this so we relax more, creating less and less drama, fear, symptoms, and conditions.

Another interesting experience in writing these essays emerged when a wonderful astrologer had mentioned to me that she was having episodes of severe nose bleeding that her doctors and even a surgeon had been unable to help her with. As soon as we hung up I wrote an essay on nosebleeds for her. Before I had the opportunity to deliver it I had connected with someone new who was actually experiencing terrible nosebleeds as well. I read her my new essay even though we had just met on the telephone. She was in awe of its resonance for her as it expressed exactly what she was feeling and the soul challenges she was currently facing. The essay revealed the changes she needed to make while spiritually guiding her and offering her the hope and encouragement she needed. A few days later I gave the essay to the astrologer and it resonated completely with her as well. She experienced the essay to clearly read her soul, and in following the advice and accessing and receiving the healing offered, the nosebleeds ceased. Months later while talking with her on the telephone she told me that her nose had begun bleeding again. I told her to reread the essay right away because she was now ready to see something new and learn more important information about herself, life, and spiritual journey. She told me she had kept the essay with her most important papers on her desk and she would certainly read it again right away. I was very happy to hear that after she worked with the essay again her nosebleeds once again had ceased.

With all my experiences doing readings for physical, mental, and emotional conditions, I have learned to trust the intuitional spiritual guidance that steers these essays. I have no medical background nor do I look up the condition before I channel or write about it. It is just something I can do just as naturally as a singer may sing, a musician composes music, or a sculptor sculpts. I have continued to write the essays because people of all ages and backgrounds have confirmed the accuracy of the spiritual truths that emerge in them. Everyone, from naturopaths to yoga therapists to nurses to psychotherapists and college professors, has utilized the essays finding them to be an affirming boost of self-confidence to help heal and transform their lives. They gain confirmation of their feelings, which are speaking for them in the form of their symptoms, and come to embrace and appreciate the spiritual growth opportunity offered by the conditions themselves.

Now you have this opportunity. You can welcome medical intuition and sacred cosmic psychology as part of your daily health regime. This self-empowering addition to your well-being can serve as a great complement to true integrative medicine because you are integrating your spirit as the most important part of your healing. As 21st century mystics and mystics in the making, we must now be open to mining the gold that lies within us as we awaken The MetaPhysician Within and simultaneously experience an even greater acceleration of our global spiritual awakening. We are fortunate to be living in such an extraordinary time on the planet and in order to explore fully we must have the right equipment. My greatest hope is that this book can serve as a sacred healing tool of discovery and awakening for you.

The more that we all call upon our MetaPhysician Within - our higher self, Divine self - the less energy we will use in creating symptoms and illness of mind, body, and spirit. Rather than making our healthcare appointments and treatment decisions out of fear, we can align with our higher self before we even see a doctor, healer, or therapist and develop and maintain a more balanced relationship with them. We will find that we won't be spending nearly as much time and money on healthcare, and our caregivers won't be so overwhelmed. As well, their energy will be freed up to do other important work. I remember watching one of the presidential debates between Hilary Clinton and President Obama during the 2008 campaign. As they spent about 40 minutes intensely focused on healthcare, I became frustrated because I knew that something could be done to radically improve our situation, something they were not even discussing, which was the financial, personal, and global empowerment that comes with self-healing.

When you read these essays, you will greatly benefit from reading them alone in your own quiet space. You may also try reading them to someone you care about who is facing one of the conditions addressed in this book, or have them read yours to you. We often do need a spiritual team for the opening, care, and growth of our souls. The human spirit thrives on compassion and love. And when we are authentically and divinely cherished, adored, admired, and cared for as a child of God and the Universe we become and remain inspired for longer and longer periods of time, until eventually we remember we *too* are God and that this is the only and ultimate goal of the mystic. This is lifelong learning we are here to do and this book is meant to support the growth of the human spirit. Remaining inspired is necessary for the healing of ourselves and the world. Earth is a school of Divinity teaching life and love and having classmates to learn, practice, and play with is vitally important. The more one heals the more they will have the desire and mission to spread love and healing, too. You may begin to find that, metaphysically speaking, just as we are one in Spirit, so too are we one in our condition, and until we are each healthy of mind, body, and spirit, none of us will be. That relates to the larger mission of this book: to take people from all walks of life and all lands and lead them into the one *Holy Land of Love* and to help each other awaken The MetaPhysician Within. Through this book we can co-create the unconditional love and openness necessary for the healing of every single condition in our world and all situations across all lands.

That healing begins with you and your individual process of tapping into and awakening The MetaPhysician Within. There are many ways you can call upon this book as a guide. I recommend reading the whole book, not just those essays related to the condition that you or someone you love, or your patient or client has in front of them. You are certainly free to accept what most feels right to you and let the rest go or return to it when you feel guided and you will most likely see something else that you are ready for. Each essay appears with little editing to keep pure the communication that was received. It is beneficial to prepare yourself before reading from the book with a few deep breaths, a short prayer, stretching, and/or meditation to relax yourself so you can open more easily to receive insights and healing as you partner with the Divine. Having a pen and paper handy while taking notes or bullet pointing to better integrate the book's teachings will also help you to get the most out of the essays. You also may choose to begin a MetaPhysician Within journal to capture the additional insights and awareness that will spontaneously arise from reading the essays. Allow those insights to flow and feel what it feels like to hear your higher self more clearly as you align yourself with the Divine. Each time you will be strengthening your own intuition. Just as with any muscle, it needs to be exercised and will become stronger with practice and over time. Eventually, as you return to love more and more fully you will become your own best intuitive healer and discover that there is no greater feeling than healing and being able to pass that on to others in your own creative and unique way.

This really is a spiritual textbook, with the essays available to stimulate spiritual conversation that will allow you to feel more alive, increase faith, and have hope, which is necessary for healing any condition of mind, body, or soul. Reading this book will help you surrender your way to inner peace so you can more gracefully heal yourself, purify your soul, and transform your mind, body, and spirit.

It is my honor and privilege to offer this book in hopes that it may serve as a torchlight, a true source of inspiration and enlightenment to help you open and evolve your soul. May it help turn your pain into passion, and help you remember who you are, why you are here, and what you have come to do. As you begin to take responsibility for your conditions and how to heal them, you really will begin to turn your soul back into the gold in which each of us was molded. More and more you will be returning to your essence...that of pure love. Pure gold.

ACCIDENTS AND BROKEN BONES

Opportunity for Rebirth and Renewal
Learning to Become Naturally Neutral – The Divine State of Being

Metaphysically speaking, accidents and broken bones are ways in which the body, mind, and soul are injured, so that one can be reborn and renewed. Most often a person who has been injured has been on a journey, consciously or not, to reach his highest hopes and dreams, and make them a reality. This individual tends to be a martyr to extreme levels at certain times in his life. He often needs help physically, emotionally, psychologically, or financially, yet feels awkward asking for help. The accident occurs as a way to force one to get the help in the area or areas needed most to help him be who he is meant and needed to be, for himself and the world.

When an accident occurs that injures the physical body, one cannot escape without it penetrating the psyche and hurting that as well. Generally, or perhaps just lately, this individual has not been listening to the call of the inner child who is most always around at the time of an accident. Usually, within a two to three week period before the injury, something of significance has been on the mind of this person. He is afraid, however, of really looking at and dealing with this particular part of himself and his life. This part of his shadow has been coming up in order to heal and transmute into the light of consciousness for the soul. There may be fear that he could be left all alone to fend or care for himself. He is having a hard time letting go of what has, in the past, been such a part of his life and level of comfort. However, as things change in one's life, so must their physical surroundings. This person is often not willing to let go of what he truly no longer needs or serves including relationships, places, and things. Ultimately, however, he must so that he can think once again more clearly and for longer periods of time. Then and only then can he go forward with his life and his higher purpose.

This individual has been very much in the dark and tends to wear thick blinders when it comes to the call of the *wild divine one* within. He can actually imprison the higher self when what he really wants to do is to dance, dream, and live life to the fullest. There is so much pulling on his spirit by the screams, silently or not, of the ego that one actually trips and falls and hurts himself a little or a lot. The degree of injury to the body, mind, and soul often remains to be seen until one is open enough about his fears and insecurities. Patience must be practiced because this could take what may seem like a very long time. Generally, this individual does not allow the Universe to support him even though he himself has done much for the Universe. This makes the Divine very sad and the higher self very angry – for this soul is not to be stifled. The frightened child within is holding on so tightly that one sometimes must collapse in order to open up fully once again and be able to renew his faith and the condition of his true spirit. Our conditions and all that we experience are purposeful and metaphysically considered necessary steps in life's journey. These experiences are intended and designed to aid individuals in the opening and rapid evolution of the soul. What is most important is how we determine and interpret this. Life is an endless study of the self and its spirit.

When a person has an accident he must keep a vigil for himself and become vigilant in light of his higher self. What he is looking for and needs most is attention from only himself. He often puts too much stock into what the experts say, no matter whom that may be in the moment of where he is, or what he is doing or dealing with in his life. The truth, however, is that this person is very often an advanced soul at the time of the accident, but does not give himself credit for this, and this is where much of his frustration lies. He is admittedly nervous about certain things, which is positive because he is able to show a vulnerable part of himself. However, this is not the highest part of himself. This individual most always knows what to do for another, as well as himself, but often he does not believe the part about knowing what is best for him. He often believes that someone else should tell him what to do with his life. In reality, however, he does not need advice, which is why he does not listen to anyone for very long anyway. What this person needs most are long rests or naps at regular intervals. He often does not realize how very tired he is, and this tiredness is what often *trips* him up, so to speak, in important areas of his life. This individual is about to discover something of great importance, but, if he keeps on trying to control his life and his daily whereabouts, and continues to support the wrong people, as well as his own ego, he will continue to suffer and create a mishap of some sort. Metaphysically speaking, he has gotten himself into a mess so that ultimately he can come out on top of his game once again in the most important areas of his life. Quiet, alone, and restful time is essential for being in one's highest self, and it is during these times that decisions and insights flow more readily and rapidly.

This individual needs to become aware that he can tend to be a little too intrigued by the lives of other people, which means then that he is not where he could be in the evolution of his own life in the way of his soul's advancement, relationships, career, etc. He may tend to put himself into troublesome relationships and situations and often may not regard the other person. This mostly occurs out of his own fear of abandonment. He is now learning to let go of those he is not serving and open the door to the many that are waiting for his game to be back on, so to speak. Now is the time to be open to new ideas, places, and people. This person is generally not one for sitting around, but again, he is one for resting on a regular basis. He is a great teacher of getting others to go slowly, but tends to feel if he himself is too slow, he may just not start up again.

When someone has an accident they are unconsciously seeking the medical, spiritual, psychological, and physical assistance needed to further the life and career of the higher self. During times of pain and turmoil it is important to sit quietly in meditation and prayer. If you're able and it feels right, kneel or ideally lie in the powerful full prostration pose and pray with desire and emotion, allowing your nonphysical teachers, guides, and angels, all of which have been trying to get your attention for so long now, to come to you freely. Not talking to others about one's mission or problems at this time is also very important so one can be clear and hear the Divine speaking directly to him. This individual has had to finally experience an accident so that this Divine connection could occur and strengthen. As one recovers he will be better than ever and off to a new way of life that has been trying to emerge for a long time.

This person usually loves to be alone, but at the same time fears this. In relationships he tends to feel that if he is not polite and nice to those he loves, they may close the door forever more. He can tend to have quite a temper and at times be very sarcastic. He does not mean to be like this and at these times he is merely acting out of the inner child who is frustrated because he is not being seen or heard in a particular situation. This person is learning how to let things go. The even greater truth is that he is someone who is not to go unnoticed, as he is needed to be the center of attention in a positive way for the greater good of all. When an accident occurs it often means that happiness is on its way, as long as one remains open to it and for the Divine to come through. And, if or when fear comes in, pray powerfully and with great emotion, and just as a child may, wish it away and it will go. A simple prayer such as, "Dear God, please replace my fear with faith", can and does work miracles. If peace then washes over you, you will have successfully surrendered your way to inner peace. This is something we each must do over and over again during our lifetime. The quicker we learn to practice surrendering our way to inner peace, the less pain we will have to create and experience.

In the light of your higher self you must honor yourself, and never put yourself last. You must learn to speak your truth and to acknowledge your accomplishments, as well as where you may feel or think you have made a bad choice, or perhaps taken a wrong turn. Metaphysically speaking, there are no mistakes – there are *choices* that have the potential to transform into great lessons, and if one is and remains very open, these can and will become tremendous blessings. You are traveling to a very vulnerable place and where we are vulnerable is always where we are hiding our own divinity. This unseen divinity often lies between our unseen wings, and it is what makes us too heavy to fly with the true wisdom and actions of the higher self. When we have an accident we often feel that we have had our wings clipped; however, the truth is that we must at times clip our own wings in order to grow larger ones. Our vulnerabilities must be revealed so that they can transmute into our strengths and our gifts, which are waiting to be honored and exposed to ourselves and the world. Without the "accident" one simply would not be able to heed their call and achieve their destiny. He would instead miss his spiritual mark and fall victim to fate. The accident must be continually blessed, especially when you become afraid. You must realize that you are not broken and you do not need to be "fixed". Rather, you are evolving into a greater soul. The accident, or rather the experience or condition, was created to serve as a catalyst so you could more rapidly expand and dissolve the mask of the ego, so you could stand and live more and more each day in the reflection of your highest self.

When someone breaks a bone or experiences an accident of any form, he or she must know that it is not the end of the world, but rather the opposite is trying to emerge. A Divine gift is always revealed as one is healed. There is so much stored in the body and bones. When one really lets go the wisdom released is plentiful. One will begin to become divinely naturally neutral to their life situation and conditions of mind, body, and soul. This is the holy space we sometimes literally *fall* to get into. To become naturally neutral is our Divine natural nature – our most pure and spiritual self and state. It is where every being is en route to consciously or unconsciously. It is the path of surrender and least resistance. It is the path to enlightenment and the meeting and being of our Godself. Our spirituality and its maturity is reflected in our ultimate neutrality and this takes much practice for everyone. We are each but spiritual beings, having human experiences for the greater good of all. We simply must recognize this truth and see and learn how each and every human condition of pain and turmoil - no matter what form it takes – can be transmuted into the light and love of God. It is our responsibility and greater purpose to turn our pain – all of our pain – into passion. True and enlightened passion is what we each have to discover as well as to gain. This is where our future belongs. There is no pain that is wasted – there is no pain upon our planet that cannot be transformed into the gold of our own.

An accident does much to alter one's consciousness to the necessary degree to match or align oneself with the higher self. Again, metaphysically speaking, there are no accidents. There is no action that does not lead to our higher self if we are open and willing to have our personal truth and destiny revealed. It is in this state of Divine Revelation where we heal. It is our birthright to heal spiritually, and as we do, the body and mind follow suit. This is our human exploration and our divination by God. We must never give the physical body power over the spirit or the mind, because reality begins within the imagination – which lies in our soul's mind. Our positive actions and thoughts are needed to heal any ailment the soul creates so that the soul itself can heal and evolve. Over the course of each of our lives we are given endless opportunities to individuate as we recuperate from any life situation or condition of body, mind, and/or soul. The more we bless these conditions and use them as both our catalyst and compass, the more we lessen our fears and simultaneously build our faithful will, which is necessary for the healing of ourselves and the world. The more we work towards this most important and only goal of enlightenment, the more we will go back to being in our pure state, and we will finally not only meet God, but know, without a shadow of a doubt, that we *too* are God in human form, and we shall honor, see, and know this in ourselves as well as everyone else. Is there anything else more important than this!

ALCOHOLISM

Allowing Spirit to Become One's Most Influential and Personal Guide
Endless Opportunity for Growth, Service, and Exploration of the Soul

Alcoholism is about discretion in one's heart. It is about going so deeply within and when one does, it feels like the war within. The alcoholic cannot stop himself from going deep where most of those around him do not travel. Therefore, in order to feel comfortable with his openness and sharing of Spirit, he will drink so that it and he will be accepted and considered fun and interesting to be around. There is generally a low self-esteem that is very thick with these individuals. They tend to feel much more loveable and desirable when they drink. Alcoholics have a strong fear of rejection always looming in their subconscious. This must come out and be revealed so that it can be healed. The alcoholic unconsciously drinks so that later on he feels badly enough about himself and goes into a very dark space; it is within this space only where he can look at himself in an honest way and have a chance of healing himself. An episode of drinking to excess then serves the higher purpose of a "mini" dark night of the soul. This is when one has the greatest chance at spiritually opening and maturing, therefore healing his condition, and then ultimately transmuting it for the greater good of all.

The alcoholic drinks to hide the pain of loneliness and what he perceives as failure in life on any level, whether that be in one's personal relationships, career, or in any social situation. Alcoholics tend to compare themselves to others and their lives, but don't often go beneath the surface while looking at others. These individuals are very good at creating and recreating self-defeating ideas and situations for themselves. They tend to always be judging another, yet especially they stand in judgment of their own soul. They drink so they can actually save themselves from the pain of themselves. They want to numb themselves of the self-hatred and betrayal, and so they drink to temporarily feel a love, an importance, and to create a nonchalant attitude as best they can.

This person must constantly ask himself before he is going to drink, *Who am I trying to impress? Who and what am I hiding from and don't want to see or be seen, so I drink to put an imaginary veil over my aching heart and mind?* The alcohol will last him for a short time. It works and gives him the time and energetic space he needs to heal on a profound level, and at the same time, a very low level, for it is through drinking that these individuals actually find for themselves love, healing, and rest from an often boring day-to-day life.

Most often in the life of an alcoholic there comes a time when he must surrender, just like anyone else, but the soul of an alcoholic is one rich in the tasting of the spiritually minded. He must be fed Spirit, and the only way he can be fed until he stops drinking is to drink. There is nowhere else he can get this high that he seeks. No one around him can give it to him. He can't find it anywhere but in a bottle. Even though it is an illusion of freedom and pain relief in the form of a drink as his technique, it works for him until it's time and his spirit says, *Enough!* He then brings to himself the highest form of love from others around him, as well as himself, and he knows he must stop drinking or lose himself completely and those he loves. The alcoholic's disguise of not standing in the truth of who he is, is enormous. This causes more pain than the drinking and all that comes with it in the way of material, physical, and relational problems. The alcoholic must come forth, surrender, and reveal himself in order to heal because God or higher self is silently, or not, screaming at him so loudly he cannot resist any longer. Something finally triggers in his heart and soul that says, *This is it! No one can do this for me, but me. I am sorry for all the problems I have caused, but that was then, this is now, and I am going to change my life, make a difference, as well as make amends to those I love, especially to myself.* This is what one learns and the lessons continue for all, not just some. However, an alcoholic can never really take a break from growing or he will end up very frustrated. He can become so afraid to drink again that he then becomes almost addicted to staying sober.

Alcoholism is believed to be a disease, but it is really a rotting of the brain that this person was given at birth so that a new one could grow. It actually does, energetically, because the alcoholic destroys his brain stem and cells to a degree that God must then intervene. As this individual builds his faith, he creates and builds new brain cells simultaneously. Alcoholism is actually an amazing opportunity to be and feel one with Spirit, as well as everyone. Alcoholism offers endless opportunities for growth and to be of service. There is also endless territory that this soul can explore, and the rewards of his life are then sweet and simple and glorious. This person can go on to become one of the most generous beings of heart and soul. Once you really commit to staying sober, bit-by-bit, Spirit will become your own most influential and personal guide. ☿

AUTISM

A Great Teacher in Learning to Become One's Own Guru
Opportunity for the Creation of a Formless and
Boundaryless Lifestyle

A utism is caused by the light in a child's eyes that has only temporarily shut or toned down, so that his or her parents, especially the mother, or any mother figure deeply involved in this child's life, could create her wings and fly on her own. The autistic child is teaching her to stay calm no matter what is going on or what is being said by anyone, especially those whom she perceives to be an authority on subject matters including autism and her own child's case. Autistic children lack the attention needed to be who they were born to be. This is not to blame anyone, especially a parent or guardian. This is to merely say that this child is not what the earth would or does consider "normal". These children come to teach, just as a child with Down syndrome or any other condition considered different than the norm, that one must go deeper and stretch their own metaphysical mind. Children with autism are teaching the lay people around them, as well as their doctors, teachers, and other caregivers that they must lay new ground, as there is much to be learned and prescribed about and for this group of individuals.

A child with this condition needs someone in their life who has the "patience of a saint". And, for those who were already quite patient before autism came into their life, they will now earn and develop even more to accommodate the child's needs, as well as their own. This child comes teaching others to not have any expectations of what "normal" may be, as there really is no normal anything. This idea of "normal" is something one has inherited by the brain and must be eradicated for healing to occur on a great scale. The child or adult who is autistic is one who needs each day to sing, dance, and play. These individuals need these types of creative activities more than most so they will learn and cultivate a necessary balance, which then often simultaneously occurs for other family members.

Autism leaves a hole in the heart of the Beloved Divine that aches and needs to be filled with love and tenderness of the Divine itself. Whatever this child and family members, especially the parents, can find to evolve their souls as quickly as possible is necessary action for them. A spiritual practice for all involved is also extremely important, especially for the one with autism who needs to have this to turn to. Rather than "act out" they must learn to go within. The acting out serves to show others how much they desire this on a soul level for their survival. In order to thrive this one needs to have a practice that they themselves have devised. This child must learn, know, and act upon the development of the growth of his or her own psyche. They are not ones to listen to authority and this actually can create much more stress for them when they feel confined to the laws, no matter how simple. They simply do not believe in them for their spirit still lives, or longs to go back to living where there are no boundaries, which means no laws and no right and wrong. Metaphysically speaking, autism is here to create the formless and boundaryless lifestyle and condition of a very high-minded and extremely enlightened individual. To spend any time at all in what is perceived to be a *holy land* is crucial for this child's development and future success living and functioning in society. There is much time that he or she must look to spend within, as this is what the autism is asking for. They need permission for their inner authority to speak. Some individuals will automatically just "shut down" so that they can heed the call of their spirit. The only way that they can hear their spirit is to shut down the sounds of the earth. Almost as a person who suddenly goes deaf is how it can be with a child with autism.

Metaphysically speaking, this condition can be cured by going to the light for the time and the fight of their lives. This is very much a condition where all intimately involved with this child's life are being asked to transform into the light of their higher selves. There is little room for ego in this experience and lots of room waiting for the spiritual, natural nature to be restored for all. The child with autism is a great teacher for learning to be one's own guru and to really know the self and God. The hole that is in the Great Heart is waiting to be filled with sand from the sleep that has permeated their sleep for so long, and now this child has come to awaken in full force to create full form at a rapid pace.

One must be careful in the ways of parenting this child or children so that they are not blinded by their own guilt, or feeling as a victim in any way. To fall into that role is to fall into a great hole that if you do not climb out of, you will drown in. However, this simply is not an option, as the bond that wants to be formed between child and parent is so incredibly powerful that as long as one prays for an answer with passion and desire, one cannot help but to hear their answer, as well as their call, and reform any and all forms of ego that have been stored for far too long. The condition of autism for all is truly a call for freedom from the burden of the calls of anyone but the Beloved in your child and yourself. And, with heeding that call your purpose of being a lamplighter for others shall be born. The call is to go as deeply as you can with the love and light of the Divine so as to penetrate your own soul and that of all those you meet in your life, so as to make the greatest impact upon the soul of your own, as well as theirs. Meditation, prayer, and deep contemplation are the greatest tools for the spiritual healing of all conditions, but especially those such as autism.

BINGE - EMOTIONAL EATING

A Tool for Releasing and Healing the Past
Opportunity for Learning to Love and Parent Oneself Properly and
Spiritually Maturely

The subject of binge eating falls in similar suit with all eating disorders. Binge eating stabilizes in a child's mind when they are rewarded and/or soothed with food in mind. This disguises the pain of what's happening around them at the time with the form of food becoming a security blanket. So, when an adult is so fixated on food, one becomes annoyed at the prospect of being healthy and doing things that are good for them rather than pacifying them.

These individuals get *stuck* at the age when something painful occurred so they began to use food as a substitute for love and affection. It is the equivalent to putting a bandage on a wound. It feels good for a short time and *covers* the injury or the "boo-boo", so to speak. Food eventually becomes the bandage for this person's emotional wounding. As one individuates into adulthood and becomes more spiritually mature and aware, there is less and less of using food as a tool for survival and love. To a child, food represents pleasure and discovery of new findings of emotions. Food disorders come in the disguise of a parent's lack of attention and affection for themselves, which is reflected in the child trying in some way to overcompensate for the parent or caretaker who does not know how to care for themselves. The child tries to mirror, but there is no mirror, so he or she uses food because of the way a child relates to food as a fix-all for most upsets. We give children lollipops for getting shots at the doctor's or for getting a haircut. We take children for ice cream for special treats. While this is at times good, one gets confused and *stuck in time* with the reasons for feeding themselves. Food is certainly an earthly pleasure, but it is not a replacement for love and affection or the best reward for a job well done.

It is the concept of getting *stuck in time* that needs to be focused on. The healing of those times is crucial for continued spiritual growth and the evolution of the soul and the attainment of its highest mission. These individuals tend to be good healers and truly enjoy teaching others, but their effectiveness of being both healer and teacher for others becomes lessened if they do not clear their times of being stuck. Hypnosis by an advanced spiritual practitioner can be of tremendous help for healing the effects of binge eating as well as any emotional eating. This is really an abuse of the self that must be healed if one is to be truly at peace in life and remain with a steady stream of work and new opportunities and experiences.

When we grow to love ourselves first and care for our spirits we mature emotionally and learn how to care for the body for its greatest good. Eating is one way a person cares for the soul. The more we mature emotionally and spiritually the less we emotionally eat. As we mature spiritually, we know the body truly is our temple and the vehicle and home the Divine works through, and we care for it as such. It becomes a natural way of life as we spiritually heal ourselves. We then tend to naturally look for the healthiest ways to care for our bodies, minds, and souls, including the ways of rewarding others as well as ourselves.

Eating disorders are an opportunity in disguise to learn how to parent oneself properly. Binging is a *holy happening* waiting to shine its light upon it. Binge eating can be alleviated as one works on healing the wounds of the inner child. As a person learns to love and parent themselves properly and spiritually maturely, eating disorders, just as any other symptom, or condition, can heal. One recuperates as one individuates. The eating disorder is the tool for these individuals and, in reality, a holy event each time they binge because they then have an opportunity to heal and shed light on pieces of their shadow. One must be open and have a strong desire to have the truth revealed as to why they are emotionally eating in order to see what they are, in fact, trying to *feed* themselves. All addiction leads to and desires unconsciously to transform into one's *holy addiction*. This is the higher purpose of addiction no matter what one is addicted to. There is a force – whether food, drinking, drugs, shopping, sex, or any other addiction – that spiritual healing cannot only heal, but can also help you to release your true passions and purpose. The *third dimension addiction* is the underdeveloped passion equal to one's intensity that can evolve into our holiest cravings and purpose.

This is all positive because with the utilization of our addictions we can transform from our human form into our fullest divine form. This is a road to our purification, which we are all on. This is the path to enlightenment and if we use our emotional eating and believe in the higher purpose and paradox of Spirit, we can heal and become more of who we really are without the packaging or baggage of excess weight.

BIPOLAR DISORDER

A Quest for Spiritual Peace and Freedom of the Soul
Opportunity for learning about Life and Love and the
Workings of Each

Bipolar disorder is about someone who is consumed with thoughts of darkness and disillusionment. Those who are bipolar slip very deeply into a place of discontentment and disorganization of the mind. This is a form of dysfunction that can be healed. These individuals are extremely out of balance and distance themselves from reality of varying degrees. They cannot see the truth and blame others, but never themselves. They feel they are right all of the time when they are in an extreme state of this condition. Inappropriate social behavior is also characteristic of this disorder. These individuals do not like to be alone and often need an audience to care for them and be there for them to blame, shame, and confuse as well. They are usually very believable in their position. They are often quite talented in many different areas. They can be quite charming one moment and then, like a snake, quickly bite someone they love very much without looking back at their behavior or trying to change it at all.

Those who live with the bipolar condition can actually heal rapidly, and some almost immediately, if they surrender truly from their heart and soul. Peace rather than chaos can be the real and more present state of their lives and minds. These individuals become very sad and can feel quite alone when they are in a difficult mood swing. When they are up they take everyone up with them and when they are down they take everyone down with them as well. Brilliant they are, and when the snow falls they get very happy just like a child. They are also often in the state of a wounded child when they act out. This is exactly why they have created the bipolar situation, which is so they could actually see their behavior because it would be magnified so large and extreme. It is often very difficult for them to admit there is a problem because they really do not see it. They are generally very bright individuals so they believe they would know if something is wrong with their behavior. They do often seek pain and time management ideas and considerations.

Those diagnosed with this condition are not at the top of their game but certainly could be if they would seek out and receive spiritual healing. To spiritually heal is what their souls have been looking for and craving all along. These are naturally very spiritual beings. All their lives, realizing this or not, Spirit is what they want to receive and give to others. They are born as natural healers and care deeply for their fellow human beings. However, they were not exposed to this type of behavior and often were the product of living in a home where children were "seen and not heard". This is what troubled these individuals most as they grew. Because of their abilities of Spirit they needed to be nurtured. They needed to nurture their spiritual gifts, but in most cases these gifts were not seen or spoken of and therefore they lay dormant for far too long. As this person grew, the bipolar behavior took form within them so they could locate those gifts that were lost.

These souls often feel they really do not matter. Almost all bipolar people need to boost their self-esteem. They tend to be insecure and this is where healing can begin as long as they are willing. They are often the type that needs to be shown things so their faith usually needs to be built as well. They are afraid of things like thinking they are sick or that they appear weak. They do not like this because the ego mind says, *Excuse me! Just wait one minute. Are you talking about me?* They can become very defensive in these times so the ones that love them need to be very careful and gentle in how they speak to them. They can also be quite tricky as well, which also makes them very difficult to deal with. There is so much projection that goes on in the life of a bipolar individual. They really believe that they are a victim in their personal relationships and try so completely and wholeheartedly to have their partners or family members take responsibility for the pain and troubles of their own mind and heart. For the others in this person's life their own primary lesson is to learn not to take things personally. This is so difficult because one with bipolar personality disorder can be very cruel at times, as well as very convincing. This is definitely a disorder or condition of the spirit in one person so that the spirit of many others can also heal. For those with bipolar disorder, to heal one must create balance in their lives more than most. They need nature, art, music, quiet time, writing, and the reading of spiritual material. Also, being an advocate for anything they feel passionate about is necessary medicine for these individuals. Injury to their own soul is often so deep that one must reach out to help others that they are drawn to. To make others happy is what they really want, but in their own frustrations, concerns, and fears, they end up creating so much unhappiness.

Often the only thing that will work for them is medication for a time; not forever, but just long enough until they get themselves on the road of really knowing themselves and their spirit well enough so that they feel safe enough and able to trust themselves to be their own best healer. This is when they can access The MetaPhysician Within so they know when, what, where, and how to heal themselves. This can take years of practice as it does for most individuals. Knowing oneself and how to care for one's own soul is a lifelong practice. However, one can use the medication until he or she slowly replaces it for meditation, prayer, and holistic practice, which they will discover on their own as they surrender and explore their way to inner peace. Bipolar is truly about life and love and the learnings and workings of each. It is a call to locate the God within oneself and to encourage them to really find themselves and believe in who they are and why they are here. Bipolar, like so many conditions and symptoms in our lives, is a gift from the Divine in disguise to get us to go finally into the direction of our soul's highest mission. Bipolar is no different; in fact, these individuals are extremely powerful because of their intensity, which is their underdeveloped passion, so when they heal, they will become remarkable individuals who can offer so much in the way of true communication and direction and dialogue with Spirit.

If, every day, these individuals could remember to bless the experience they are in and surrender from their heart every frustration, they will heal. When the spirit heals there is nothing more to do, nothing more to seek, and nothing more to gain. This condition is a quest for spiritual peace and freedom of the soul. Because these individuals are filled with repressed passions, they must create something as extreme as what is currently called bipolar disorder in order to discover those passions. And one simply must be quiet and relaxed and feel free in their minds and hearts in order to create those moments of ecstasy that they are striving for. It is within those moments, collectively speaking, in which their condition will eventually subside and not only heal itself, but transform itself into a healthy and balanced condition of peace and service to themselves and all of humankind. ⚕

CARPAL TUNNEL SYNDROME

A Time to Let Go of What No Longer Serves the Soul
Opportunity for the Imagination to Run Wild
with the Mind of the Divine

Carpal tunnel syndrome affects those who have very high standards for themselves and others, and the trick to their healing is to not be so hard on themselves or those whom they respect and love. There is an outward niceness to these individuals and they are most certainly lovers sent from the heavens in order to create in new and old-fashioned ways, but they tend to have a hard time changing gears, which allows them to do something new and exciting. The fears held within hold these souls back. They tend to have a deep fear of failure for any new projects and are afraid to move forward in the good and right direction that their souls are leading them. The carpal tunnel then develops as a way to force them to do something new or at least to entertain the idea. Otherwise, these individuals tend to get locked too deeply into a routine, which forces out the young, playful one within that not only seeks but needs to dive into something new and explore other realms they are not too familiar with in this lifetime, but in other lifetimes, most definitely. In this life, he or she has come to excel and master what was begun in other lives, which cannot ignite unless one begins the task of loving themselves into the surprise of their lives.

Spiritually speaking, this is a very exciting condition, as much is held within these individuals in the way of their feelings and their truest thoughts of the commitments that they made long ago to others, as well as themselves. This is a situation where one must go through old relationships, jobs, cars, homes, or anything that is part of their lives and/or their "stuff" and seek to separate what they feel they love, need, and can't live without, as well as sorting through and letting go of all else to those they know, and perhaps those they do not know. This is a way to "clean house" so one can remember their past and all that they know and carry from their past into this life. Clearing all in their lives that no longer serves or helps will aid this one in their new ventures. These individuals must have clean plates and clean and clear minds. Therefore, some form of meditation is often crucial for those that develop this condition. Carpal tunnel is also about being addicted to things that are unhealthy for them, and they are seeking with their symptoms to rid these and transform them into their holiest addictions at this time in their lives. There are certain actions, people, places, foods, and behaviors that all need to be reevaluated. Once this is done, which is not an easy task; new opportunities will remarkably and miraculously appear to them and those that they love, as they are very much souls who travel in packs with other souls who are like-minded.

The reason carpal tunnel exists is because those who attract this condition do not get enough mental stimulation in the areas that they truly crave and this is where they must search. That is, in seeing more clearly what and whom do they really love, and where they can serve the world most efficiently utilizing their gifts, which they will discover further through a more serious meditation practice. There is so much to gain for and from those who have carpal tunnel syndrome, mostly in the area of self-improvement. These souls are often born leaders, as well as counselors to others. They are often very supportive individuals and secretly wish they had the kind of support that they offer to others for themselves. Much enlightenment can be gained by this type of behavior because if one is conscious of their thinking only then can it be elevated to higher standards of the soul who is capable of receiving much more in the way of the catapulting and the evolution of their souls. The place they must always remember to come from is one of courage in the expression of their feelings. Never sway a decision because you do not want to offend or hurt another. More appropriately for this individual is to think deeply before they speak and only when they feel it is utterly necessary, as sometimes these souls can really confuse another or put someone off with their sarcasm that is actually a truth but can be felt as irritation. So proper placement of words and the energy behind them is being asked to be looked at and considered and perhaps adjusted within personal relationships. This is good advice for all human beings, but as stated previously in this particular condition, this is where a great focus could offer tremendous growth and make these individuals even better communicators, as well as counselors to others, which is very much needed now on the planet.

Carpal tunnel is about a time stuck inside when one tried to hold within who they were, and this is often a carryover that is necessary to clear. This is achieved by spiritually healing the self with a considerable amount of meditation and deep rhythmic breathing. While they do this the insights for clearing will come into their consciousness, and only when this occurs can this time be cleared.

The unseen message with this condition is to be brave. Be brave and have the courage you need to be and do something quite different from what you think and have been doing. This is a time for your imagination to run wild with the mind of the Divine. And, if you ask with passion and desire for the Divine Mind to come to you, so it shall and give to you all the direction and insight you need to discover your path and where your next turn shall appear and all that you can do to speed up your process. All the healing that you so freely give to others you must make your own as well, and do the same for your own soul. Your hands and wrists and arms are crying for the love of you and looking for some inner hugs and tenderness that only you can give to yourself.

CATARACTS – EYE CONDITIONS

Learning to Look More Deeply Within in order to See the Godself
Opportunity for Spiritual Exploration and Depth

The problem with those who are having problems with their eyes is, in quite simple terms, that there is a deep loneliness of the Divine within this person's soul. There is a small part, about the size of an eyeball that has energetically clogged the heart of this person. It is important to note that this can also clog an artery one day, as well as affect the eyes. This individual's vision is distorted when it comes to the Divine and its view through their eyes about themselves. They are wonderful when it comes to seeing God in others, but the problem comes when this one no longer sees the Beloved in themselves, and it is primarily in this area that the person with a cataract, or any type of problem with the eyes, must look at very deeply and carefully.

There was once a time in one of this person's lives when he or she was extremely poor and this affected their family. Such guilt and shame was put upon them that they chose not to see some things, as this was the only way they could find peace. They were riddled with guilt and fear of survival, but mostly for their family. They did not love and nurture themselves and because they felt very inadequate in taking care of others, they could not give to themselves much at all. This condition is mostly, therefore, a carryover from times gone by, but the work of loving and nurturing the self is still looming behind their vision, and it is in this area where most of their spiritual work now lies.

This person tends to put others' feelings and also thoughts, as they are very intuitive beings, ahead of their own. They tend to merge with the desires of others and often lose the true dreams of the soul of their own. They must go very deep into themselves and their connection to the Divine and then, and only then, will they heal more of their spirit that was left behind. There is always a tiny bit of thought of being left alone and without family that clouds the vision of the higher self. This person must really work on rewarding him or herself for a job well done as often as they can. This is quite a beneficial exercise for them as they seldom do this for themselves. There is also a question they must ask themselves about the way(s) in which they would like to serve in the world; but first, they need to ask what it is that they love to do and how they can make that service. These individuals are often very good teachers, but something in their personality can turn another off to this part of themselves, which is the part that is insecure in their connection to the Divine. Others can see and feel this from them, yet this person is not quite conscious of this; thus, the cataract is created so that he or she looks deeper within, behind the scenes, so to speak.

This person is being asked to look behind and beyond the mask. They must see the beauty as well as the dark side of themselves and others and learn to not run away or ignore this shadow side. This person has a natural gift of seeing in the dark, meaning they are able to see the shadow of another, which is the unhealed not the unholy side. They are able to point it out and help others to then heal a part of it by transmuting it into the light of the higher self. This person, however, is not as effective as he or she was meant and destined to become at this. He or she must work passionately and very dedicatedly to this cause. This is crucial for their own spiritual healing as well as achieving the highest call and cause of their destiny. It is within one's own strength of connection with the Divine that they can connect most efficiently with others on a holy and more profound level, and it is this that this soul desires and seeks most.

Individuals with cataracts or other eye problems sometimes confuse times gone by, as in the case of past lives, where they can see more value and put more importance on the material and physical world of themselves and others. However, the deeper and higher truth of this person is that what they really seek is the gold of the Beloved. They seek this true and most real gold more than many of the other souls around them. This one must, therefore, keep on mining, and in their mining they shall not only retrieve this gold, but will find that within this treasure are the keys and laws of the Universe. They will then open to levels of love they did not remember existed.

Spiritually or metaphysically speaking, this is a very exciting condition as there is so much opportunity for the growth of many people in connection to this person. If he or she dedicates their life first to themselves and the Beloved Divine, they will radiate this wherever they go and many new gifts and wondrous connections shall appear to them.

This person is learning to wear their heart upon their beautiful sleeve, which needs to occur, as they tend to be secret about their truest feelings. This is because they fear rejection and harm on a psychic level as well as the physical and material world. This individual is now going deeper than ever before and must relax, breathe, and remember to pray to replace any fear with faith all day long if that is what is called for. This is one who loves greatly, and once again, their work comes in the form of loving themselves, as well as to organize their life as such that they are as free as they can possibly be in order that they are able to fly off on a dime and live as spontaneous a lifestyle as they can. These souls desire freedom and they want desperately to explore and roam the ethers, which is exactly what waits for them in the form of much spiritual exploration and depth.

A great healing tool for the individual with any concerns or situations of the eyes and obstruction of vision is to really look at their eyes. Talk to them and ask them, "What do you see and what do you want? What is hiding beneath the cataract that I need to look at but have been afraid of letting someone, including myself down?" There is so much opportunity in talking to any symptom or condition and asking, "What do you want from me? How can I make us freer from this situation? How can my spirit heal, as I deserve to heal? I am but a child of God's and I wish to see that in myself as well as everyone else."

Symptoms are God in disguise, so one must generate communication. They are clearly the unseen equipment leading all the time towards the direction of the soul's deepest and greatest calling and the full achievement, potential, and realization of one's destiny.

COLITIS

Learning How to Care for Oneself Without Guilt
Opportunity to Replace Ego Consciousness With That
of The Christ Consciousness

Colitis is a very difficult condition to heal physically because individuals suffering with this tend to live in secret of their innermost feelings. They try to be open and honest, but have tremendous fear of success, as well as a fear of rejection blocking them. There is often a painful feeling in their heart that they can be discarded easily by friends and/or especially family members if they do not perform in the way they feel is appropriately desired by others. This person's heart and soul also carries grief not belonging to them, but rather that of others who have walked the holy life in other lifetimes.

Those with this condition have much consciousness of the Christ, yet are shy in expressing this wisdom. As they grow they mature even more conscious with the Christ energy, but do not feel free enough to pursue their own dreams when it comes to their highest and most holy mission. They allow others to, or have been led astray by those who have had the most influence in their lives while growing up. These individuals were generally not focused on the Christ consciousness, but rather that of the ego. This is, or was, not intentional or negative; it simply means that those raising this child had parents who lived in fear of being recognized as the Christ energy themselves. Often, one or both parents had difficulty in expressing their deepest feelings, so they kept them "in check" as well as in disguise.

A common, weak quality in the personality of those with colitis is that he or she is not afraid to be shy and feel it's almost good to be this way. They are often in turmoil about wanting to shine or stand back in the area of their spiritual life. This side, however, does come out during a crisis and/or when it feels safe to speak their truth. Most of the time, however, this person does not feel safe and quite often hides their most holy side, causing them the most trouble in their body, mind, and soul. The colitis serves as a guide for them in order to reveal when they are hiding their deepest feelings. They are trying so hard to not expose themselves that they lose control and often, rather than expressing themselves verbally, *attack* themselves with an *attack* of colitis. Those with this condition often blame themselves and have guilt about things they need not because the situations they most often feel guilty about have nothing to do with them and everything to do with those closest to them. These souls cannot bear to see certain people they love suffer, so they feel through their own bodies and process the emotions of others, as well as of themselves, through the symptoms of colitis.

These individuals tend to have many people around them who are similar to themselves; however, it is healthy for them to also seek out the most opposite personalities they can find and see what it is like to live the way these others do. Investigating other lifestyles is wonderful as is trying whatever things these others do that they feel particularly curious about. The person with colitis often does not want to try new things and is quick to stay in a pattern of the same people, food, locations, vacations, work, and play situations. They are not the ones often looking for something new and exciting because they are among those who can be happy or content doing the same thing for long periods of time. It is often others they live with or are friends with that make them feel alive and encourage them to try new things. This is not easy for them to do, but it is possible and important in self-healing. Being different is such a part of who these individuals are on a soul level, and when they explore new realms, ideas, and territories is when they will be ignited on a soul level. This "ignitement" must occur; otherwise he or she can get stuck for much too long a time with others around them and then become the target of their inner aggression and frustration.

These individuals are quite jovial at times – happy on the outside, but on the inside often angry and/or full of rage, although not sure this is what they are feeling. He or she tends to feel very frustrated, but the truth is they are incredibly angry at any mother type in their life because they feel too stuck to them emotionally and energetically. What they are not aware of is that the opposite is true – they are not connected enough to the women in their lives, as they would truly like to be. Not a phony "have to have" relationship, but one of true joy, where time spent with the women in their life is that of peacefulness and joy. There is a lot about the relationships with the mother, sisters, and wives of these individuals that must be worked on, but first they must admit this to themselves. There are issues of familial bonds with the one who suffers from colitis. This is a problem and condition of a soul who is not satisfied with their life as it is and tends to blame everyone, especially the females in their life.

These individuals need the most help and healing with the feminine side of themselves. This Divine Feminine is the Christ energy in its purest form. It is extremely important for healing of the mind and body – soul and spirit – that this person comes to terms and agreement with this energy within their own psyche. It will never be enough for those who suffer with colitis to live a semi spirit-filled life. These individuals can be wonderful healers or many other spiritual-type individuals, but first they must recognize the self of God within.

There was once a major crossroads in this person's life when someone they trusted, often one of religious nature, misled them. Because of the hurt caused by this person, the spiritual life of this sufferer shut down, creating a drama of painful *letting go*. Things became so difficult to let go that the only way they could be free from the emotional pain was to create the condition of colitis so they could painfully *let go* physically of what no longer serves them. Healing occurs in the higher vibrations; therefore, one must strive to remain in the light of the higher self, working towards this on a daily basis with the only goal of becoming an enlightened and purified soul.

It is very helpful for these individuals to journal each time they become angry. In addition, it is important to relieve pressure on the bladder as often as possible, as this area is also affected by the anger and releasing of its pressure on the psyche. Watching happy and funny movies and listening to deep music, especially classical, can also be very healing. If one does not enjoy classical music, just playing it softly in the background can help in raising one's vibration. The unseen world of classical music and its harmonious spontaneity and healing vibration will greatly increase the chance of the deep soul soothing necessary for healing. Deep therapeutic touch in the way of massage by someone carrying much of the Divine Feminine energy will give the body the safety it must feel in order to let go of what no longer is serving. Prayer and regular communication with the world of Spirit is also being asked to advance in this soul at this time.

Lastly, these individuals need to organize their life the way only they would like it to be organized. They tend to get very frustrated if their personal space is not in the order that they like, yet they are conflicted in wanting to please others simultaneously. This is a natural stage and reflection of personal growth. When this person gets to the point where they truly love and care for themselves first without any guilt, the colitis manifested in order to teach this greatest of lessons will no longer have reason to exist and will disappear. One must remember to *bless* the colitis, just as any condition or life situation that is co-created with the soul, so as to receive the attention needed so the body does not need to be in tension in any way, shape, or form.

CROHN'S

Learning to Light the Flame of One's Own Heart
Opportunity for Realizing the Ultimate Divine Mother Within

Crohn's comes from the left side of the brain and not being in it enough. It is a condition affecting mostly those who are stronger in right brain functioning because of their upbringing and conditioning, as well as the inclusion of all of their fears. Crohn's is a way to release a very painful past – one where a child felt very sad about not being seen for how special and loving they really were. The mother, and sometimes both parents, was very much within her own shadow most of the time and this is where she mothered. Her states varied with others from higher self to lower self. However, when it came to mothering of the most basic conditions she was very insecure and inadequate in her own mind – no one else's really – but in her own mind she had major issues of feeling worthy enough to mother a child that was often quite more evolved than herself. She could feel the child's intensity and needs, yet knew she could not fulfill even one of them most of the time. This made the child very sad, as well as herself. The child felt the needs of her mother and forgot those of her own.

Crohn's can heal if one becomes an *Ultimate Mother*. These individuals are often very mothering of others, although, not always their own children, but others such as friends, associates, clients, and neighbors. This person can help just about anyone who has a problem - and will often try and go to great lengths to do so - almost to the point of smothering another, but most always out of love and seldom their own needs. They are looking to replace the mothering that they did not receive. When one completely forgives the mother that they did not have, the condition of Crohn's will heal and they will be without dis-ease of their heart – the sadness that penetrated all the way into their system – the most private and sensitive system of the body, with the most important function of releasing what is no longer needed, but was so needed at the time. Like a mother and the child who grows and one day needs her no longer, and they become the mother to anyone who will let them mother them.

Now this person must look deeply into their own eyes and see how beautiful they are and see themselves as their own newborn, toddler, adolescent, teenager, etc., until they are fully grown and able to love themselves the way they unconsciously continue to seek from just about everyone they meet. There is something this one is always missing or judging. They are feeling more like they are *missing* in relationship to another, but the truth of what they are *missing* and most likely will not stop missing is the love, kindness, tenderness, and care from a mother who was emotionally not there. She was there physically, most always, but energetically, the mother was often somewhere else or wishing that she was or thinking she was missing something in *her* life; what she was missing was the mother of herself as well. She never learned how to love a child of God's. She never felt worthy of it herself. She felt more embarrassed by what were silly things to most, but to her were very important. Often, economic situations, career, or lack of what others have or what others were thinking, was going on in their mother at the crucial time of the early years of those who now are suffering with Crohn's.

People with Crohn's must learn to light the flame of their own heart and not look or wish for another to do this. It will never work and this can never be faked with these individuals, as what was given to them because of their life in the womb, and then when born and for the next important years, was the development of an incredible radar of what *is* truth and what *is* fear in another. These individuals cannot be lied to, although at times they do get stuck in the "wish of the child" of having a loving partner, but really what they are looking for is the loving mother, the loving friend, or the loving family member. They need to now become this to themselves. It is important for them to remember that if they had had this mother love they would not be nearly as intuitive as they are in adulthood and these children are needed to grow and mature into teachers and healers of great accord and they will settle for little else. So they have and/or had the perfect mother for their future. Their mother was tortured internally and often it did not completely show. They were ones with a great façade who wore a wicked mask at times.

Those with Crohn's must do a clean sweep of not only their physical space, but also of the right side of the brain and start anew, giving the intuitive side of themselves the most important attention their spirit deserves and is demanding by offering Crohn's. This is a situation and experience where one can learn tremendous amounts of information that does not come from a book, teacher, healer, or friend – not even from the most amazing and attentive mother in the Universe. It comes from themselves – deep in their heart and soul waiting patiently to come about and out. So when there is a flare-up of Crohn's, know without a shadow of a doubt that you are in desperate need of some attention and love in the way of the Ultimate Mother from yourself and no one else in those moments of your life.

Crohn's is about learning self-healing techniques. It is about being in your truth and not making excuses for yourself or anyone else. It is about opening and relearning what you shut down, which is your own intuitive deepest sense. You shut it down partly for protection because you did not want to know the truth of your environment and also because the Ultimate Mother within wanted to give it all away to the mother who gave birth to you, but could not see nor feel the gift you were giving her. She could not be grateful for you or celebrate your life the way you are about to be able to do for yourself. She was a wounded soul who came to you to give birth to you so you could feel and experience the pain of separation and then one day realize and actualize the Ultimate Divine Mother within yourself. There was no other way but for you to learn in this way, as this was the divine design, which you co-created with the Greater Divine. Without deprivation of "The Mother" you would never have had the opportunity to actualize and experience the ecstasy and feelings of the Divine.

The condition of Crohn's in its simplest of forms is resentment that must be released in order to find the deep inner peace that your spirit is seeking to rediscover – and so you shall. You must envision yourself in your highest of self with your arms wrapped around your birth mother and speak your truth so you can release your peace and let go in the way that is more appropriate for you now that you are ready to individuate into your full adulthood. Tell yourself that you are there for yourself no matter what and you will always be. You must promise yourself that you will unconditionally love yourself first and foremost so that you can truly love others (especially your birth mother). This is the most difficult relationship to heal, as it is seemingly the most important to a person having the human experience. But spiritually speaking, the greatest gift of health and healing comes when one is in touch with their innermost being, and that *being* forgives and loves without conditions, every being under the sun.

Without questions and without rhymes, one must learn to love the self and then they can love all else, including the mother from which one was raised. She served her role well, she created you, and it was in the deprivation of her own soul that you were granted a well that would never run dry of all the love that you were denied. The Ultimate Mother within us is, in reality, the same as The MetaPhysician Within, which is the God within as well. In all different ways and with all different vehicles, every human being must eventually awaken, realize, and actualize this being, and then their most holy work can be completed.

CUTTING

Opportunity for Deep Soul Connection with Self and Others
Learning to Transmute Self-Inflicted Pain Into Unconditional Love

Many of those called cutters today are actually old souls who cut themselves (partially) because they are remembering – on a cellular level – lifetimes gone by where cutting was a form of celebration or an initiation into the world of Spirit. The act of cutting was considered an act of bravery during that time. Those who cut themselves today are spiritually wounded, but are, nevertheless, brave souls who do so in a futile attempt at remembering who they are and who they were in another time, as a warrior or priestess-type person. Although it's a difficult concept for some to understand, all of our lifetimes are rolled into one. As with the cutter, there can often be a *bleed-through in time* that forms part of what is currently going on with us in this lifetime. Cutting must be more fully understood psychologically and caught up to today. Everyone is bringing their past, present, and future into the now space, although many do not know about, believe, or understand this (or other unseen realities) about the metaphysical world. Cutting is a perfect example of a bleed-through in time, but there is much more involved with this condition.

Men, women, and often young individuals cut themselves for enjoyment, satisfaction, and/or excitement. Some become euphoric as though drugged during this act of self-mutilation. Cutters cut themselves so that they feel pain, which keeps them connected to a world filled with the pain of others. Those who cut are very often advanced souls unconsciously looking to connect with those on a lower vibration than themselves. This actually becomes impossible, because as long as they cut themselves, they cannot connect fully with their higher selves; this, in turn, prevents them from truly connecting with another. They cut themselves to feel the blood rush out of their veins so they can, on some level, cleanse themselves of impure thoughts. They punish themselves for simply being human and having very human thoughts. Many of these individuals have not yet built up the self-esteem necessary for self-forgiveness.

People often cut themselves to get to the truth of what they perceive as a seemingly meager existence. They tend to feel quite small on the Earth plane, but the opposite is true. Those who cut themselves have extremely large spirits with very large missions to discover and act upon. However, without healing spiritually, it is often impossible to achieve one's highest purpose. The experience of cutting actually prepares them in developing the compassion needed in order to heal and serve others. To cut oneself is akin to an act of self-crucifixion and is performed so that one can experience the sensation of resurrection. The act of cutting is about dying (without actually dying) and then experiencing a Christ–like experience of coming back home, feeling that perhaps they would have another chance at life and living it more fully.

These individuals can also be quite arrogant in their thinking. They can emotionally harm the ones they love most, but whom they have the hardest time expressing that love to. As they torture themselves, they are often equally paining others, especially those closest to them. They do not yet realize this and cannot do so until they understand that, for them, in this lifetime, cutting is a form of self-abuse that neither society nor they themselves will tolerate.

Although cutting is a form of self-punishment, it is also about self-adoration. It is a convoluted way of adoring and even adorning oneself. The cutter must be in contact with a professional who has performed similar acts, so that they can relate on a deeper level. This deep connection with another is necessary for this soul to heal. They need to be seen beneath the mask they wear and be recognized for the spiritual being they truly are. In this way, they can recognize the Godself that is often hidden deep within them. A spiritual healer or mentor is essential for this individual because beneath the cutting lies a human being trying desperately to be born again and return to the love that they are trying hard to remember. This person becomes so frustrated in their state of remembrance that they want to *cut* away the shadows rather than appreciate, learn, and grow from them.

Those who cut themselves sometimes secretly want to cut another person in an effort to share their love and ritual. This is quite dangerous because it can become addictive and can also perpetuate their condition by having a *partner in crime*, rather than one in the light. These individuals are also usually very competitive within themselves and will keep cutting until their souls become so tarnished they cannot and do not wish to function in society any longer. It is important to mention again that cutting was, at one time, and for some still is, considered an honor in some places. For such an individual, there has been a mix-up in the *dialogue of Spirit* in this time and place. Those who cut themselves are invariably unaware of this, but revealing it to them can certainly help them understand a big part of why they could now be hurting themselves. This can be very healing and transforming information for many of these souls. This individual is a seeker of truth and wants to know the *unseen world* and how it works. They want the truth to the bigger questions of life, and, one way or another, they will receive the information in which they desire and need most.

These souls will quite often also cut themselves out of boredom with life. They feel, *There must be something more than this. There must be something happy and joyful for me that I could care about.* Of course, there always is, but one who cuts themselves has so much inner turmoil inside of their soul he or she easily forgets such things. It is helpful for them to keep a journal where they can delve deeply into their emotions and the underground world so they can permanently release. They tend to have a considerable dark side (the unhealed or shadow side), but within that darkness always lays the "goose that laid the golden egg". One must often go through the darkest of times to see – and become – the light of the Divine.

This person needs tremendous understanding. The last thing he or she needs is criticism on any level, even about their cutting. They need enormous compassion, which is difficult for them to receive from others because who they are and what they do is so difficult to understand and/or relate to. This person is not quite sure why they are cutting themselves other than for the thrill of pain and the knowing that somehow beyond the pain lies the wisdom and courage needed to grow into the higher self and the person they will become. If cutters receive spiritual healing, they can end up serving and helping their community (and the entire world) enormously. Those who love them must remember what they need most is to be understood, rather than judged, for them to have a very good chance at healing and transmuting this self-inflicted pain into proper unconditional love, care, and soil for their personal spiritual growth and maturity, which lies there germinating and waiting somewhat patiently to be born. Their soul needs more tenderness and care as they are often like an exotic flower or bird and must eventually learn to treat themselves and others as the same.

When these individuals cut themselves they are in some way trying to discover the truth, which is very important to them, as again, they tend to be truth seekers. They are souls who can speak their truth more easily than most, and the difficulty they experience is that most of those around them do not want to hear that truth. Sometimes cutters can enjoy seeing those they love, as well as those they do not know, hurt themselves because they can then finally feel a connection to someone else. Even though it is not a positive connection, it is still connection and deep soul connection is what is craved. This is rare for them and its absence is devastating to their psyche. These individuals must find ways to have healthy connections with others, which will happen when they become more connected to their own higher selves. One of the best ways for them to do this is to be in nature, as this is the purest connection there is, a place where they can speak their truth with ease and pleasure.

Journaling and speaking their feelings into a recorder are also wonderful for the healing of the spirit, as they are, through their cutting, trying to hear the voice of the soul. In hearing their speaking voice talking to themselves and God, much emotional movement will occur, which then always follows healing. They can even become addicted, in a positive way, to hearing their own voice, as it is one of power, truth, light, and love. This takes time and a continual spiritual practice. As these souls are very original beings, they must develop their own best regular spiritual practice, and if they stick to it, they can grow beyond their wildest dreams.

FIBROID TUMOR

Opportunity for Realization of the Soul's Expression
Learning to Live Life According to One's Highest Vision and Dreams
as an Artist of the Spirit

Metaphysically speaking, fibroid tumors develop within a woman's body when the time has come for her to let the world see who she really is; yet, being so afraid to leave behind the "baggage" or wounding she came to earth with, she holds onto her pain in the form of a fibroid. She can be so deeply lonely on a soul level that she tries to unconsciously comfort her psyche with the fibroid, as though holding onto a baby that will never be conceived. This "baby" in reality is her unrealized dream for herself – not the dream of another, but hers alone. The fibroid forms to allow this woman to hang onto something, even though it is not what she truly desires; nevertheless, it is something to hold onto. She temporarily and unconsciously settles for a fibroid tumor, rather than a baby, based on her own dream and the way she envisions preparing to serve God and humanity.

The fibroid forms from many layers of abuse of the self, as well as the acceptance of emotional abuse from others. As well, if not in this lifetime, certainly in previous lifetimes, this woman has been the recipient of much sadness and turmoil. Once removed, however, the fibroid or fibroids take with it much debris of the psyche. When she has had time to recuperate and return to her spiritual center she is much more able to see and act upon her deepest dreams. She can then realize what she has long suppressed in the way of her own soul and its expression.

This condition is telling you to not forget about you! The fibroid(s) will torment you with its symptoms and growth until you can no longer look yourself or another in the eye without the truth being told. You most always are living in such a way of being – as "the keeper of the peace", to the point of losing the truth and wisdom of who *you* really are. Sadly, you tend to give away your power, which is your inner peace, quite often. You are, of course, one with the Divine; however, you don't always see yourself as such because of the way you seem to disappear whenever conflict arises. You disappear in an effort to keep the peace as well as to hold yourself back. This mechanism of fear actually then manifests into one or more fibroids so that, eventually, you will not be able to ignore the voice of your soul or its greatest dreams and mission.

Fibroid tumors can also manifest when a woman is looking outside of herself to make something happen for her. There tends to be too much wishful thinking without enough action, so the tumor forms and grows as *surrogate action* of the soul. She advances then in the way of growth of something – if not the higher self, the *tumor self.* This woman can also become attached to the tumor and at the same time despise it, which usually is reflecting one or more of her personal relationships. Each relationship she has and how it is affecting her life and the health of her spirit, mind, and body must be deeply meditated and focused upon. Every single relationship in her life that is truly valued must now be reevaluated to see where changes are desired and need to come.

This same woman does not like to see anyone suffer except, perhaps, (unconsciously) herself. The fibroid develops so that she can look again, deeper still, into her own heart and pull out the sadness that holds her back from speaking her truth. Some part of her is afraid to be seen for who she really is and what she really knows because she knows others may be frightened of her, or will no longer feel comfortable around her. She often has much natural intuitional guidance streaming towards her, which could more comfortably flow through her, but this higher knowing is partially blocked within the fibroid. And because of her hesitation to develop this part of her psyche, the tumor develops as *surrogate psyche.*

The woman who forms this type of tumor is generally spiritually gifted and is often in the process of turning her own light into the light of others, usually for those that she has known longest in this lifetime. There is much occurring in the way of *empathic parenting* of others, and not necessarily that of her own children. She can actually trade places, in a sense, with these other souls in her life so as to not have them suffer. This often occurs because she is a strong warrior of Spirit and really desires to help others. However, she is actually hurting herself by using her own life force energy rather than using that which comes straight from the Divine. This energy can easily be channeled through her for others without losing or hurting herself, but she does not yet clearly understand this concept of healing. This means then that she is unnecessarily using (and losing) her own light, which drains the creative energy she needs to have her own dreams and visions come to fruition.

Often women develop, manifest, or create this condition so that they are literally forced to do something for themselves. The spiritual gift being offered to you through the fibroid is the eventual cultivation of much integrity, peace, and harmony. You are learning to be your own best guide and live your life according to your highest vision and dreams regardless of what your partner, relations, friends, and/or colleagues may think.

When a woman experiences this condition she also tends to become very brave, and is initiated into higher forms of love, wisdom, and spirit. The trick or key is to remain forever in the light of the higher self, and this is where much practice must come to fruition. This connection to the higher self and God must develop so she, in fact, can achieve her dreams. Without this strong connection she will continue to use her creative energy to create things that force her, rather than naturally develop, and turn into reality for her. This *forcing* is what is most unpleasant in the way of symptoms.

It is also very important to honor the workings and development of a fibroid because it is often the catalyst for one to ultimately take the proverbial bull by the horns, joyously and with a sense of humor, and go for what she believes and truly wants to achieve. The fibroid, spiritually speaking, ultimately brings the courage and sensitivities needed to allow the light to shine through its shadow. When this happens and one is healed of spirit, mind, and body, there is then no stopping this creative individual from being the *artist of the Spirit* that she came to earth to be.

FIBROMYALGIA

Learning How to Ride the Wave of the Emotional Body
Opportunity to Own One's Power, Breathe Fully, and Release the Past

Fibromyalgia comes from a wound set deep in-between the legs and the heart – a wound of emotional and sexual "baggage" or scarring that waits to be exhaled by the *volunteer* experiencing this condition so that they may stand up for themselves, finally assuming complete control of their emotions and heart and owning their healing sexuality. Fibromyalgia is pain from emotional trauma set deeply within the tissues of the body. The way out of this condition is to look forward to the gold beneath the pain that this person is discovering all on their own.

Fibromyalgia is about standing up for oneself and owning one's power, as well as wearing one's heart on one's sleeve. The person with fibromyalgia has so much compassion for their fellow human beings that they think on a small level, meaning from the lower self or the *little one within* that if they take on the pain of the world there will be less of it for others to bear. The higher self, however, knows itself very well and eventually, sooner rather than later, this person will discover that this is neither the way to heal the self nor the way to heal anyone else. This person is learning to do things from the higher self and fibromyalgia is a gift in that it is the teacher of how to love oneself. This person is a very sensitive soul who needs to show the world just how sensitive they are, not by taking on suffering, but rather by speaking from the beautiful heart they were given at birth. They came to earth equipped to handle much transformation for themselves and others and truly are a lightworker, which is a healer and/or teacher of Spirit. In fact, anyone with any form of disorder of the skin, muscles, and/or tissues is one that the world is waiting for to come into their own. The way their compassion is learned is through pain and humility. The suffering only continues because there is something in their personal computer from the pain of the past that is jammed and needs to be released.

Breathwork is essential for those carrying this type of pain. This condition is mostly an illusion; although the tissue can or does become inflamed, it is most often a manifestation from emotional pain and suffering unrecognized to the one experiencing it. It is unrecognizable because the pain is buried so deeply emotionally; creating fear, and finally, acceptance of an illness that does not really exist. Many people have been and are still being labeled with fibromyalgia. Some are simply accepting it, and finally others are concluding that it is an unacceptable diagnosis. Doctors and caregivers need to explain to the one suffering why they are feeling the pain and how they can naturally relieve it. These individuals need to know that their symptoms of pain will continue screaming into their minds and bodies because they are in truth messages from the Divine, as well as from their nonphysical guides waiting for them to pay attention and begin to clearly see what they need spiritually that will lead them to the calling of their soul and the real and deeper meaning of why they are here and what they are to do with their lives. It is crucial to find out where these individuals need spiritual and emotional, as well as physical and mental healing, so they can fulfill their purpose and achieve their destiny. Pain comes to us so that we do not miss our spiritual mark. We each must become much more astute and open to the hidden and often secret language of the soul.

The pain experienced by those with fibromyalgia most often comes from relationship issues, from those they have loved and lost, as well as those who have confronted them and they have ignored. There is a lot of unresolved anger and hurt with these individuals. To allow the pain to pass through them is essential in taking away the pain. Those with this type of disorder are amazing in that they must always become, finally, the captain of their own ship so that they can eventually teach others how to do the same. It is this teaching and healing of others from the higher self that will give these individuals some of the greatest pleasure in their lifetime.

The way to treat this disorder of Spirit, as well as soul, is to work the mind and body very tediously. They cannot waste time. Relaxation time is also crucial, as is love and affection in the ways of self-healing, massage, gentle touching, and caressing of the body by themselves or another. Mostly, however, when one is given the *Divine message* of fibromyalgia one is being offered in the way of symptoms a very powerful message to breathe and love one's self and body so much that they ground themselves into believing and knowing on such a deep level who they really are spiritually and why they are here now in human form. They will learn how and understand once and for all to love themselves first so they can teach this to others. Anything in the way of grounding will be helpful for these individuals – anything that is through the mind with the study and learning of Self and Spirit. Exercise, healthy food, making love, dressing their wounds, so to speak, in the way of movement, cooking, loving, art, or any creative act whatsoever is what is emerging and helping those with such uncomfortable symptoms to release and keep them focused and in the moment. It is important to mention that the condition called Attention Deficit Disorder (ADD) is often found in these individuals as well; therefore, it is essential for them to remain alert, purposefully and creatively busy and consciously breathing fully.

The breath of these people is often crushed in the spot of their heart's wounding. It is very sad for them, but they have to learn how to let go of the past and ride the wave of the emotional body. There is an eruption within these individuals that must be looked at, but not necessarily explored too much rather simply observed, without acting out of misplaced anger, which is in the form of pain in their body. The pain is there in a way to place the anger of the emotion on themselves rather than others, but it is unrealized and must become conscious or self-realized. Personal insights must come through this ordeal. No one can "fix" or heal you but yourself. We can help one another, but when something this deep is present only you and your own connection to the Divine and the Spirit world will heal you completely. It is about not blaming anyone or reacting to another who has caused you pain, including yourself. Many with fibromyalgia go to the place of self-punishment in the way of pain in the body so that they can feel the pain of the emotion somewhere, but they need not direct it at themselves, which is what they are creating. They need to know that they can breathe through it and focus. Simple yoga poses can greatly support and help one to release the pent-up emotion that is anger being denied. Often, we do not find it acceptable to have negative feelings, but it certainly is. We do not have to react and hurt people or yell and scream at anyone, but we do need to feel it and it can be made more simply exorcized through the body with activity. However, until one acknowledges where and why they are angry the symptoms will persist. This is a way to consciousness, but not necessarily the best or easiest way to get there. Quiet and alone time works wonders. Yoga and deep breathing as well helps you to find your center so that you can embrace the pain and breathe new and fresh life into yourself and your body and mind so that your spirit can fly once again and the soul will be soothed.

We do not have to feel such excruciating pain because we were taught to not cause any trouble and to "not rock the boat". It is all God - the light and the dark. We cannot have the light without the darkness. We cannot create, experience, and be the light without the recognition and acceptance of our darkness. The way of the warrior of Spirit is often through the temples of hell. The way to our own heart's desire is to walk through the fire burning in our bodies for what sometimes seems like an eternity. We can become so frustrated and think we are to varying degrees depressed. But, we will overcome this, too, and we will stand and hold our own hand and know in the end that we were never alone and we can get through anything now because we have learned the oldest lesson of the ancients and mystics. To love oneself is to love others and the way to living pain free of mind, body, and soul is to look to the heavens and see and embrace the gold waiting to be discovered.

Fibromyalgia is a way for love to unfold for ourselves so deeply that we create miracles wherever we go and forever more. Love is always in the air. Breathe and breathe, and breathe deeply and deliciously while you look to the heavens and ask for nothing more but to serve and live freely and happily. To choose the way of peace all day and every day is one great lesson of this and all conditions of Spirit. The Spirit calls us so loudly and will never give up on us, which is precisely why the symptoms persist. Spirit loves us so much it will never give up on us. And, in this lesson, we learn to never give up on ourselves. We must know that we are always there for ourselves. As well, there are no bad feelings; rather, they are each laced with the gold of the heavens. We are not bad people for feeling anger, resentment, or even revenge, we just have to practice letting these feelings pass with the ease of our breath and always remember that we are not human without these feelings. We cannot learn to unconditionally love ourselves or others without the dark feelings of hate and anger as well. All the great healers, teachers, and masters of Spirit have felt these feelings and have had to learn these same lessons. We are each as one in the arms of only love.

INSOMNIA

Opportunity to Reveal and Surrender Areas of Control in One's Life
A Time for Opening New Doors to Learning, Loving, and Self Care

Insomnia is a dis-order of sleep and those that suffer with this condition are often very similar or equal to those who suffer from sleeping too much. Metaphysically, this means that it is the same disturbance in personality creating either sleep condition. A person with insomnia often suffers from trying too hard to heal the world and generally not focusing enough on healing him or herself. Their mind tends to be quite busy and they feel that they have so much to do that they cannot understand why, when it is time to sleep, they cannot. There is actually some arrogance with those who cannot fall and stay asleep in those moments in that they feel that they are not entitled to rest like everyone else, because they have so much work to do. There is, therefore, an issue of self-importance that needs to be explored as well as the lack of faith involved with true insomniacs in order to improve and heal him or herself.

Some individuals rarely sleep and are merely resting when they think they are sleeping. It is very difficult to live in the mind and body of a truly advanced insomniac. Almost everyone will, at times, suffer to some degree with this condition. Insomniacs sometimes go so deep into their subconscious during the day that they simply do not need much sleep. Lots of people can function on four or five hours of sleep and some can even survive with only three. However, there is an eventual breakdown of the personality as well as the physical body for most of those with sleep disorders. A person needs to sleep because this is when they are actually learning, healing, and loving - truly efficiently and unconditionally. When one sleeps is when one is really most awake. Metaphysically speaking, sleep is when one is studying and remembers much more than they could possibly absorb or have access to when awake. It is a much different and more sacred place that we each travel to when we are asleep. We are then traveling astrally and there is a great deal going on; we visit those we love and have lost, we travel beyond time and space. We travel to other planets and we learn new skills. When we are in deep sleep we are very much in the consciousness of the Divine, which we often find difficult to be in when we are awake and functioning on the Earth plane. We are in a higher dimension while we sleep and this is when our spirit is communicating to us, utilizing our dream state. Therefore, deep sleep is crucial to the development of our psyche and the maturation of our spirit. It is especially important for those with insomnia to sleep because this is exactly the place they need to go for healing and the effortless learning they will receive while they sleep, rather than struggling to access what they unconsciously know they can receive from the sleeping world. Since they cannot sleep they then try to accomplish the same while awake on the Earth plane, which of course, is impossible to achieve. On some level they are aware of what they are missing in missing sleep, and they try desperately in their waking hours to over accomplish and achieve.

So how can one induce sleep? One of the most successful healing forms for insomniacs is hypnotherapy. Hypnosis is advised for anyone who really has a problem falling and staying asleep. Another way is to practice yoga, stretching and breathing for 20 minutes or so and/or soaking in a sea salt bath before bed. A nighttime ritual is very important for all levels of insomnia. Also affirming (out loud, if necessary) to yourself that you will have a wonderful and restful healing night's sleep before you go to bed will help. Lighting a candle and listening to soothing music, especially that created with sound healing techniques will generate a peaceful atmosphere. Eliminating television, computers, and/or the reading of any material except that which focuses on positivity, spirituality, love, peace, and healing is advised. Journaling before bed for a few moments can also help release the built-up tension that can tend to keep one awake. A person with insomnia must take seriously his or her preparation for a healing and nourishing night's sleep. It is hard work, especially for those who suffer with this, to prepare themselves for a good night's sleep because those are the individuals whose spirit is really calling and needs them to sleep very badly so that they can do all of the above and reach the levels of consciousness while they are sleeping, which they need in order to achieve and learn what they are struggling to learn, consciously or not.

Insomnia is the voice of the soul, in that one can only go for so long without sleeping before having negative effects in every area of one's life. There can also be a lot of confusion for true insomniacs because there are so many choices to aid in sleep. Again, naturally, the path of yoga, deep breathing, and hypnotherapy, etc. is best. However, at times a sleep aid in the form of medication is necessary so that one can break the cycle of not sleeping. Caution and consciousness must be used while taking prescription medication because sleeping peacefully and waking soundly can be very seductive, thus leading to addiction and postponement of more natural healing forms that can lead more easily and readily to so much positive growth and change. The higher purpose of insomnia is to hear the voice of the soul in its language of the silent screaming of not sleeping, to encourage one to go deeper within him or herself rather than the psyche of another. In knowing oneself thoroughly a person will not only find themselves and God, but will eventually find everyone else as well. There is so much joy one will be able to connect with while awake when they experience the joy and release of passions while sleeping. In essence, a condition of insomnia is about struggling with control in certain areas of a person's life. These areas must be revealed and surrendered so one can heal and enjoy having rewarding and satisfying sleep on a regular basis. ☿

IRRITABLE BOWEL SYNDROME

Opportunity for the Creation of a Well Balanced Life
Learning to Cultivate Boundaries, Protection, and Self-Preservation

Irritable bowel syndrome comes from the part of a person's brain that goes into remission of his or her true feelings. This is, however, impossible to accomplish because the body is preprogrammed to confront these innermost feelings speaking for them in the form of symptoms. The resistance to explore their feelings comes from a deeply hidden fear of abandonment by those they love, as well as, themselves.

Often times, people with IBS allow others to go in front of them in the *line of life* and then later on regret – in the form of IBS – their over and unnecessary helpfulness stemming from a neediness and/or greediness of Spirit and its use. Learning how to use his or her spiritual gifts of healing and teaching in the appropriate space and time, with the right and good individuals to receive their gifts, is very important in eliminating the symptoms of this condition.

Individuals with IBS are likely to be annoyed with those they love and know quite well, yet they cannot admit this to themselves, let alone the others involved in their life and condition. Those they love irritate them, and as well the lining of the bowel becomes soft and tender and therefore irritated, too, serving as a form or vehicle of *letting out* their true feelings. Although painful, this is the only way they have learned to cope. Those with this condition generally do not have enough fun on a daily basis and need to deeply relax and really "let their hair down", so to speak. This is especially the case when symptoms begin. At these times one must stop all work to focus a few moments on deep breathing, allowing the release of the toxicity being picked up from their environment, including that from those they are in contact with.

There is also a *letting go* of unspoken ideas, dreams, and conditions, which this person finds right, good, and acceptable to their own soul. People with IBS generally focus too much on what others need and desire and not enough on what their soul is screaming for in the form of symptoms. The symptoms say, *Enough of this stuff – let me out of this situation with you for it is not mine to heal – I can support you, but I will not process your stuff* (which the IBS is doing). The bowel is working overtime being too much in favor of another and not enough of its own, so acting out as a screaming child saying, *Hey! Wait a minute, what about me? Can you not see I am suffering here?* This is not the job of others, however, but rather of the self, especially having to do with boundary setting, and in some cases extreme boundaries must be set.

IBS is about boundaries of the psyche, as well as learning and practicing self-protection and preservation. It is about doing exactly what it is that *you* would like to do. For example, if it is dancing, dance, singing, sing, or acting, act! This is a condition about the child within not having enough fun doing what he or she truly desires to do. This individual is also often struggling with the "should haves" and the "would haves" in life, which must be eliminated for recovery of body, mind, and spirit. It is also time for this person to explore, study, and/or focus on their true calling in this lifetime. This person, however, often feels lost or stuck in the way of their deepest feelings when it comes to the Divine and their direct connection and outward expression of this. He or she eventually does come to terms, but most often it is in an unconscious way, as they suffer so much with symptoms rather than surrender to the Divine and its mysterious ways (meaning *surrender* your way to inner peace). Usually, this one is very stubborn when it comes to communicating directly with the Divine and often looks to people, books, or whatever or whomever they consider to be the experts in the area they are currently interested in leading them consciously or not in the direction of the Divine and its plaintiffs. There is no other way that one can let go of their past(s) than by describing and inscribing for the Divine. Right into action this person must go, especially if they are consciously on a spiritual path. Younger souls and/or those who are physically younger may not understand this fully; however, if they continue to follow their dreams literally and figuratively they will begin to conduct themselves in a manner more conducive to their own healing.

Those with IBS often find it overtakes their life and love, draining them and creating much fear. They must learn to consciously breathe as often and for as long as they can each day. Deep, long, stretched out breathing techniques work wonders for this and just about any condition. However, IBS is one that is so much about tension in the heart manifesting in the area of letting go and correction that breathing like this is essential in bringing together harmony within the body, mind, and spirit.

Lastly, this individual tends to be fearful about having their own heart sing, but can be generously and incredibly happy for others. It is now time to begin and continue for the rest of their lives to heal and teach themselves, just as they are so wonderful at doing so for those they love, as well as for those who simply cross their paths. These people have so much to offer and so much to receive in return. It is important to note that receiving can be so difficult for them that when it comes to Spirit and true love they tend to live alone, not having as much social activity as they need for them to heal and release completely from the physical hold. It is important to remember that the way is very often to play and making this a regular part of one's day is crucial in achieving and maintaining balance.

KIDNEY STONES

Opportunity for Release of the Old in order
to Allow Space for the New
Learning to Utilize Prayer and Service as One's Greatest Allies

Kidney stones stem from the condition of one's mind that lays stuck in the child's mind and heart. This person has much inner turmoil yet to be uncovered, and so suffers tremendously in the letting go of heartbreak from long ago. The parents or parent of this individual have suffered tremendously as well, yet they took it out upon (sometimes in the form of physical abuse) their children. The parents felt very misunderstood and unappreciated by the children they bore. These children, however, were often left alone to care or fend for themselves. At times it was as if they were living in a charade and the parents could actually be overbearing and seemingly protective, but this is not the true case. The parents of the one now suffering with kidney stones were often told of stories that were not true when they were young so when it came time to raise their own children they often could not be present emotionally and the child then felt abandoned or abused. The kidney stones form as a way to resolve the deep-rooted anger and indigestion almost, of a loss of what their fantasy childhood would be like in their eyes.

The kidney stones represent where they have allowed their heart to close to others. Often this is with one or both parents, as well as one or more of their children. They may find this very difficult to admit and/or understand, but the truth is these individuals are of considerable spiritual power, and if one is not working consistently on their spiritual independence, growth, and maturity, they will *grow* this knowledge within kidney stones that represent where their hearts have grown into stone.

This is a very difficult condition to decode because many of these souls do so many different things. It is not an easy condition to pinpoint. The way you can do this is by having the patient do a deep study of themselves and their patterns. It is important as well that they must never judge. For these individuals, working on non-judgment is the first place they need to start looking and it should be the last thing they stop working on in this lifetime. Therefore, this person needs to learn and cultivate patience and the management and healthy release of their anger. Often, they are afraid of their own anger, which reflects their own life circumstances and where they are still fearful and lacking in faith. This person's greatest ally is service and prayer. Finding wherever they can serve others and stopping frequently to pray and make their daily life a prayer is the way this one will most quickly and efficiently heal.

This person is one not to share their feelings or their "stuff" with too many people as they feel a tremendous lacking in the area of receiving love from those that they love. They often overly mother those close to them and then in the same breath say something like, "Whatever you think is right, that is the way to go." So, they can often be confusing in their conversation and hold other people responsible for their own negativity, thus holding themselves and others back from personal closeness, connection, and growth.

The manifested kidney stones replace the love that was not shown to them. The stones actually represent a hardening of his or her personality, as well as their heart. Their soul is telling them in a very loud and painful tone or scream that they are not willing to be unloving to anyone, especially themselves. This person often feels they are not of value. They feel they are the one to do the giving and that is their job and they will take the crumbs of life. What the kidney stones are saying is, *Wait just a minute here and look at me!* Take a long look in your own eyes and see and know who stands there looking back at you. You should only ignore the voice of the ego in another. You must learn to recognize this voice and practice not allowing yourself to be energetically pulled or sucked into the ego of another. This is your highest work and that is to be all of who you are wherever you go and remain conscious of and in this state.

The kidney stones also represent to this soul that they are worthy and they want to release their hardened and wasteful ways. They want not to judge or be judged. They want to love deeply and completely and know positively the essentiality of this. They want to win at the *game of life;* therefore, the study of metaphysics, journal writing, and/or any other self-healing technique should become a priority and practiced on a regular basis. They must reveal their most true and deep feelings of grief and any other type of pain they may be carrying. These are often extremely creative souls lacking the confidence to journey with their highest vision. Often, they do not allow themselves to dream, as they feel not worthy of their greatest dreams. They settle for too little. They must work on their worthiness issues by helping others to value themselves and show them that they are worthy. This is an important part of their highest calling. These souls tend to make great counselors and leaders, often in the spiritual or psychological arenas. They also often make great scientists and teachers.

Kidney stones block the horizons of the person's spirit. When an attack is coming on one must know that the *contractions of love* are beginning and another piece of their soul is about to be painfully born. However, it does not have to be so painful. Any prenatal breathing technique will work wonders in delivering the stones with less pain and punishment of the body. This person punishes themselves by developing and creating this painful condition. They do this because they punish themselves for having bad or negative feelings for those whom they love. If this one is angered he or she is able to hold a grudge for a very long time and this is also what adds to the problem and pain of the condition. Holding a grudge is something they need to work on, as well as speaking their truth with fluidity and consciousness. If they practice always being in their truth, or at least having the intention to be in their truth, then one will heal. The more one prays to be real and have the truth revealed, the more one will actualize as well as spiritualize themselves into their highest self in this lifetime.

These individuals tend to be old and very loving souls. They appreciate the littlest gifts and compliments. They treasure the moments when they feel needed and appreciated. The trick or the healing comes when one can make themselves feel this way without anyone else around. The true loving of oneself and the true holding onto one's own hand is the way this person can heal him or herself. This condition is most certainly not a pleasant thing to experience and often so painful one wishes to be taken to the other side for reprieve. This is one who has in the past, meaning past lifetimes, suffered greatly as martyr and as missionary. Not easy roads has this one had in the past of pasts, but, in this lifetime, the kidney stones are going to be a release of the old and the allowing of space for the new to come into view.

Those with kidney stones will replenish all the pain that they have endured for the greater good of all and replace and transmute it for much personal enlightenment and love to be shared by all. The most important thing to anyone is the discovery of one's Godself and this person is one for doing so in great ways, and they will gain much understanding of the world and its people when they have fully healed.

KLEPTOMANIA

Opportunity to Access the Love Available on the Deepest Levels
Learning to Expose the Soul in a Healthy Manner

The metaphysical reason behind kleptomania and why it exists is because these individuals need to be seen in a way where they are a complete and naked soul, which means when a person is in their most pure state. Kleptomania can be a very embarrassing condition in the eye of the collective or mass consciousness, especially true when one appears to "have it all" and yet, steals. However, what this person does not have is the love available on the deepest level of the naked soul. This love is exactly what the individual suffering with this condition is starving for as they reach to take something not belonging to them or which they have not purchased. He or she reaches for the object as a replacement for what is truly desired. On some level it is known that they are reaching for something out of their own soul's reaching. In the moment they are simply overwhelmed – grabbing at something, almost anything, not thinking of its value – but rather there is something unexpressed in them where they desperately need to be seen and heard on a soul level. This is how and why these individuals risk embarrassment and/or humiliation to the degree of standing naked with their worst secret exposed.

Rather than healthy exposure of the soul, this person exposes themselves in a very unhealthy way if only to themselves – if, in fact, they do not get caught. On a deeper level, each time a person steals they are giving themselves an opportunity to heal this part of their shadow, which is the most unhealed part of the soul under which lies all the gold of one's own beneath the shame, guilt, or any other negative feeling or life situation. There is always a gift behind any condition of mind, body, or soul, and it is up to the individual to mine for this gold, dig it out, and claim it as their own.

It can greatly aid the person with this temptation, that actually moves to the physical act of stealing, †to stop for a moment and ask themselves, *Am I feeling alone in the world or am I feeling loved?* When feeling alone, they grab for something, anything that can be called their own, as they had not much to call their own in the way of behavior and often grew up mimicking the behaviors of those they loved and lived with. There was not much focus on this child and he or she often was or felt very much lost in the shuffle. In order to put on a bandage, rather than a necessary stitch, to heal the wound of their soul, they steal something, giving it a patch, but not a true or permanent healing. This theft heals or soothes them for a moment or two, and for some it can offer relief all on its own, lasting a few weeks or even months.

The actual stealing stems from long ago as a child wanting to be picked up and held. It is so frightening for this person to feel unloved and untouched that they grab things without asking or paying for them so they can conjure up the feeling of what they believe they missed in the past and still feel this way in the present. There is a sense of being robbed of something, but they do not know what it is and do not wish to explore this "missing out" feeling when something triggers the emotion in them. Rather than go deep within the psyche, they steal something, creating a bandage for the soul instead.

It is the inner child who steals, not the higher self. Those who steal are often sensitive souls in search of their own and rightful belongings. They are searching for the ones they love to love them back no matter what (including any horrible habits they believe they have). These individuals desire and are desperately searching to feel unconditionally loved by others, and most especially and importantly, themselves. To experience the feeling of loving and being loved deeply is where this person desires and needs to travel and explore. Sadly, the feeling or high received from grabbing something not belonging to them is like *grabbing* a hug from the ones they love. For kleptomaniacs it's all about love – spiritually speaking, it's all about love for all ailments and disturbances.

The personality of the kleptomaniac is one who can offer a hand and then quickly pull it back. The *kleptomaniac within* is offering with its condition to heal this part of their personality, which is being mirrored for them in the act or form of stealing something. They are stealing from and punishing themselves first. It is a pattern being repeated on some level, and patterns are meant and divinely designed to be broken, as they are spiritual lessons yet to be mastered. One must try and work to understand, not merely suppress their feelings, as the soul has many ways of being heard in order to spiritually heal itself. A kleptomaniac often enjoys hearing him or herself speak, but when someone else is speaking and they don't like what they are hearing they will retreat. The condition of kleptomania serves the soul until a person grows beyond the point of being insecure to the thoughts, words, and feelings of others.

Kleptomania is healable, just as any condition can heal in Spirit because all conditions are created or manifested for spiritual healing of the self, others, and the world at large. This person must come to terms with themselves on a soul level, especially when not feeling proud of him or herself. They must recognize the parts of themselves they are ashamed of and work to change those behaviors. Stealing is the ego's attempt to take back its power, which in reality, is one's inner peace. Similar to an impulsive child, this person grabs something not belonging to them because not only does it temporarily give release to the soul, it aids the ego in determining *its* purpose on earth of being scolded. As children, these individuals were often scolded for being naturally passionate and excitable. They were stifled by the authorities, which were the adults most present in their lives while they were young.

Kleptomania can be a very sad condition in that it is quite often difficult to reveal. The one suffering with this often creates an entire fantasy world in their mind. When this person steals it is a way for them to soothe their long suppressed soul. As children, the natural nature of these individuals was spontaneous and carefree, but they were, in fact, stifled. When they now steal something, somewhere in their minds they are rewarding themselves for being quiet and shy, the way they were not born to be, but learned to be by not wanting to cause any trouble. In a way, as adults, they still want to have a good time but not get into trouble.

Kleptomania is a very sad condition as well because mostly one is in secret a lot of their lives. The feelings held within this soul are able to release themselves a little bit when something is stolen. However, the deepest desire for these individuals is to be able to express themselves on the many deep feelings they tend to have about the world at large and the crime that goes on in a very large way. The inner child of this person is usually afraid to express these feelings for fear of being seen or misinterpreted so they take or steal something to relieve the psychic pressure that they feel from not acting on and realizing their mission in the highest way, meaning from the full adult perspective and insight that these individuals are most often able to connect with and when healed spiritually, most certainly will be able to do so and quite creatively. These individuals are also on many levels of high intelligence and are often artists, but the way that they think on the level of the collective (which is very much not who they really are) blocks their vision. This is true for many, but these individuals especially. The love they feel they are missing will be discovered when they achieve more and more of their mission in life. As well, these individuals need to seek ways to explore their creativity. No matter what it is that they may be doing, these children of the Universe are able to really tap into some exciting projects, but they must be willing to let go of the feeling of being owed anything and begin to look to give as much as they can and as often as they can. It is in this feeling and resurrection, so to speak, that they will soon find more joy than they can ever remember having and one day will even be able to speak openly about the shame that they have experienced and some may continue to live with. It is in the healing of the spirit and sharing with others that all shame will relinquish its hold upon the soul.

NEUROFIBROMATOSIS

*Learning How To Become One's Own Best Company
Opportunity to Access the Truth and Courage of the Higher Self*

Neurofibromatosis is a condition that is not very well explained or understood. Metaphysically speaking, it comes from very tiny cells in the body that are malnourished emotionally, physically, and spiritually. Individuals with this condition spend much too much time in their brains and not enough in their hearts. They tend to be very book smart, but rely much too little upon their intuition, which is actually the stronger part of themselves. The diagnosis of neurofibromatosis is the key they need to open themselves to the wondrous life that Spirit has designed for them, yet they cannot seem to find enough time in the day for normal activities, never mind the spiritually obvious and most important ones needed in the ways of meditation and contemplation. Deep contemplation of these souls is being asked for. The little cysts form pockets of low self-esteem that are being drawn out into the open so that the individual can replace these pockets with the truth and the courage of the higher self within.

Individuals with neurofibromatosis have much fear of the future and where they belong in it. Much of this fear can be alleviated along with the cysts if they would focus on the highest mission of their souls. They are being asked to really step up to the plate and find the time needed to create the space for them in the Universe. They care too much of what others think and live much of their life in the past. The cysts erupt so they can no longer hide in the mind of the inner child and expand the consciousness of the higher self. One must, and shall, grow to major proportions.

When other people are around those with this condition they can feel a negative energy and at times be afraid to just sit and be with them, so the individual with neurofibromatosis can feel neglected, discarded, unneeded, and unloved. However, the negative energy that people are misinterpreting from this person is really the fear of their child within and his or her need to please and to be accepted by someone other than themselves. This behavior, though, will never work because it forces one into an even deeper coma, meaning that they stay in an unconscious state that will perpetuate the cysts and the progression of this disease. These individuals find something about themselves that is ugly, that is not good enough, and that primarily comes from not loving the self on the level of the adult. This one must dive deep into their greatest pain and greatest fears, and when they do, the cysts may really completely disappear. However, this takes time and much inner work. Neurofibromatosis is a very stubborn disorder and can be literally in one's face most of the time. It is a very frustrating condition because it is generally not very well explained or understood which generates a greater sense of hopelessness and concern.

One can heal this condition by really looking within and studying themselves by utilizing journaling and meditation techniques. Really learning how to be one's own best company is crucial. Dancing and bringing joy to themselves *by* themselves is incredibly healing and empowering. They must prove to themselves that they are worthy of love and they must learn that it is the Beloved above for which they are on the hunt. One must never look to another to give them what they have yet to be able to fully give to themselves.

Those with neurofibromatosis can achieve endless energy and learn and grow tremendously from experiencing it. Neurofibromatosis offers so much in the way of enlightenment, but one must be open to all possibilities, especially in the area of property and possessions. Do not under any circumstances feel envy of another, but rather seek to be inspired by all others. Find something, anything, that you can see as good in another, and tell that person so. Doing so over and over will help the swelling of the ego that creates the cysts for the soul to be able to grow. The higher self works with the ego to create all healing necessary. We each have our cross to bear (visible or not) and that is what holds the key to release the peace within as well as our gifts that we must make manifest. If we did not have the symptoms we would not have the gifts. They bring us to our Maker before it is time to pass on. This means to focus on ways to merge heaven with the earth. So while there is still time one must seek to find the gold and the God within.

Individuals with neurofibromatosis would find great relief if they practice a lot of compassion for themselves, as well as those they feel to be their spiritual enemies, as those with this condition have some of their spiritual vision clogged in the cysts created. When love and compassion are practiced, a spiritual pressure is lifted and relieved and the peace within is released. They are filled with a feeling of healing and completion and this penetrates the cysts naturally relieving the body, mind, and soul. ⚡

NOSEBLEEDS

Opportunity for True Spiritual Independence
A Time for Intense Self Introspection and New Ideas and
Teachings to be Realized and Shared

When a person's nose bleeds, what is being called for is intense introspection into their life. The deepest desires of the soul are asking to be brought one or two steps closer to manifesting one's dreams. This is a situation where the individual must go deep within their own psyche and resist the need and desire to go into others as deeply as they normally would. The nose bleeds to assure that this person does, in fact, do this introspection of him or herself.

Nosebleeds are a very distracting condition and one that needs to be looked at with a fine–toothed comb. The little bugs (like small worries) in one's life desire to be made manifest and sorted through. When the nose bleeds it is time for solutions to be found. It is through the blood of one's own that the soul becomes purified enough to be an even better vehicle and source for others, as well as themselves.

Nosebleeds come from the past of having too much to do and not enough time to reflect on what is truly joyful for themselves and their lives. When this condition occurs it is time (if possible) to begin planning some sort of a vacation, preferably in a far off and/or exotic location. Those who have nosebleeds are actually quite exotic creatures, but don't indulge nearly enough in their exotic ways as they would like. These individuals often carry much joy and are very open people who like to see those they love having a wonderful time. However, when others are not in the best place this person takes much to heart upon him or herself in order to make things better for them. When the nosebleeds come they must look to see what is right under their nose in their own home that is causing them to perish in their own view. This one does not care to be the subject of conversation or criticism and would often like to be left alone, which simply is not possible because these souls are most often in great demand and this demand is exactly what creates most of their frustration. The nose bleeds to show and say to the world and themselves, *What do you want from me, blood? Well, then, there you have it. Look at that!*

There is also the condition of particles in the environment where this person spends a considerable amount of time, that energetically affects them in a negative way and areas need to be rearranged. The movement of furniture, especially one's desk, workspace, and/or kitchen areas, so as to allow and create different views, is very helpful. There is also an energetic balance that must be found between work and pleasure. The exotic nature must be fed or *it* will show you how your heart is bleeding right through your nose so you don't miss out on this part of your soul that is desperately trying to be born into the newness of your space in your life.

Nosebleeds come from a deep lack of satisfaction in one's work. Although this person is not actually or fully aware of this yet, they are getting much closer to changing things and/or expanding something in their lives. With the nosebleeds come some feelings of loss of accomplishments, but the truth, metaphysically speaking, is their bleeding is greatly serving as a role of a menstrual cycle. There are certain things no longer needed for the progression of this person's work because new ideas and teachings must now be experienced.

These individuals are often visionaries, yet they look to others for their vision of themselves. They are their own best visionary and now have the opportunity to understand this more fully. There too is lack of confidence in the area of true spiritual independence and this independence is now asking to be born, explored, and eventually passed on as they teach others.

Nosebleeds are a somewhat dramatic creation of the Divine in that the blood is quite symbolic in many cultures, religions, and ceremonies. It would be very helpful to explore these ideas so as to obtain new and fresh insights, which is exactly what the soul is craving at the time of bleeding. While the person bleeds they are actually seeding and plowing the way for many new ideas and teachings to come through them, which then can be written about and taught to others. These individuals want to experience Divine connection with other people in a much deeper way than before. They have held back in this area for quite a while and are now ready to take on more of the heart of the world. The ego resists this natural progression of the soul so the nosebleeds materialize to accelerate this process. It is a not so gentle way of making sure one does not miss their spiritual mark.

One must recommit to Spirit about their studies, teaching, and healing of the self, as well as others. The discovery, or rather the rediscovery of the poet within, is trying to emerge and through their bleeding the past is cleared so that this can occur. Although this is in quite a disconcerting way or vehicle, it is one of great efficiency. As well, the bleeding represents heroic actions from the past reenacting in the near future. These individuals also tend to be deep thinkers and like to swim with those who resonate on their equal vibration, and as well, with those who go even deeper than themselves in the way of the mystics and ancients so they can discover more of this part of themselves.

Whenever an individual is experiencing strange or uncomfortable symptoms of any sort, he or she needs to stop what they are doing and pray for assistance from the higher self, their guides, and angels so as to decode the messages held within the body, and, in this case, as well the blood. There is always a sacred message, especially when blood is penetrated and expelled from the body. This is a significantly spiritual symbol and one needs to explore their own meaning and their own psyche as to what the symbol of blood may mean to them personally. Then it is appropriate to bring in the historic aspect of the symbols of blood as well. This will stimulate further insights and ideas waiting to be triggered, remembered, and finally, appropriately utilized.

OBESITY - OVERWEIGHT

*Forgiveness of Past Hurts - Letting Go of What Does Not Serve
Opportunity to Begin A Revelatory State Necessary for the Proper
Care and Feeding of One's Soul*

O besity is something that comes from within and shows without because an individual is not really accepting what has happened to them during their life. How can one get rid of something if they do not even know or accept that it is there? The weight is a reminder for them to not forget to work on their own spirit, as well as everyone else's. Unexplained weight gain usually happens over the course of time – precious time that one perhaps is wasting by holding on to the past without letting go. Actually, it can be a fear of letting go of the past. Healing obesity is about an individual going within and *really* looking, clearly seeing, and feeling one's deepest and innermost feelings. The reason the weight piles on them is very simple, the weight makes sure they are aware of themselves, and until they *lighten up* on the past the weight will not come off. Those who can put on excess weight to the degree of obesity are very powerful individuals.

What has happened and what is being asked is that these individuals have to really come out of their shells. They allow others to control and run their lives. Actually, they let others *stuff* them. They stuff themselves with the emotions of not wanting to "rock the boat". They tend to rejoice in strife and do not let others help them. They say they want help, but most often do not want anyone to do anything for them beyond what they themselves can control. It is being a victim of circumstance. But are there any victims? No, there are not. There are, on a metaphysical level, only volunteers. We are, in reality, each a student of life and love. Quite simply, these souls feel they are there to be seen and serve and do not honor themselves enough to tell another if needed to "take a hike", so to speak. They often become pushed around, whether they realize it or not, as there can be various degrees of subtlety involved. They rejoice unconsciously and unwillingly in feeling left out because sadly, a part of them, which is the younger self, believes that is where they belong.

Obesity occurs when one person loves another and the other person (they feel) does not love them. What one who is overweight needs to discover is more of him or herself and God. Obese people usually have a great desire and intent on God and service. They dedicate themselves to love and to their families, but do not reach out much further because they feel they could then not cope with all the demands of life. However, they do need to expand their territory, as this soul is crying out for its expansion and higher purpose. They build demands on themselves and create an energetic barrier around them in the physical form of weight so that others who might really be able to help them cannot. They are silently with their weight saying, *Please stay away from my heart because I am not worthy of your love; therefore your help from your sincerest being.*

These individuals must replace the weight or the darkness or shadow with light and then the weight will magically disappear. They will literally become lighter and lighter as they open and grow and mature spiritually. They should envision their bodies becoming lighter and lighter as their real true soul begins to open and evolve. Simultaneously, one's fears will begin to dissipate from their psyche and more energy shall be *gained* to do what they would really enjoy doing most creatively and purposefully. They must take quiet time to reflect and let go – let go of everything that is not serving them and forgive everyone that has ever hurt them. Light beings are just that – *light beings* – and we were all created like that, but the gift must be seen. The gift of the darkness or weight must be blessed, accepted, and learned from, and then it can be released simply and easily along with the past. Some things such as this condition, which seems for many so great an issue for so very long, can really be quickly and efficiently healed once the person sees who they really are with their *own* Divine eyes and the spiritual healing needed is allowed to penetrate their soul. Almost as if they have given birth to their true selves and then there is no reason to *carry* anything that which no longer serves the human body or psyche on any level.

These souls are so often precious hearted and only need others to mirror the divinity of themselves for a long enough period so that they can, in fact, open their own heart and see the world through the eyes of the Beloved. When they do this they will begin to see how deeply loved they are waiting to be loved, and once this revelatory state begins for them there will be no stopping them in the care and proper feeding of their souls and most holy being. ⚕

OBSESSIVE-COMPULSIVE DISORDER (OCD)

Opportunity to Practice the Vital Law of "No Controlling"
Learning How to Naturally Surrender Into the Flow of Life and Spirit

The condition called Obsessive-compulsive disorder is about disorder, meaning things being in disorder in one's mind that are seen with the eyes, but really is an illusion. OCD is a form of discontent within one's heart. This person can be very disabled when it comes to their feelings. Their truest feelings tend to come out in the form of a release in the way of repetitive thinking or focus in one or more areas of their life in which they have yet to make peace with. Most everyone will likely be able to relate to this condition on some level, as most have or have had a touch or more of this themselves, and if not, they will most likely know someone with OCD, as it is extremely widespread. Its symptoms also often lie in deep disguise or hiding. There is opportunity to learn so much, especially in the form of compassion, from knowing and/or living with individuals who suffer with symptoms of OCD.

It is often not easy for many of these people to walk the road of their life, especially in more severe cases. They are often very much connected to Spirit, and many could be on the level of genius in this area. However, in most cases, the fears carried in this area are great. This person will not give him or herself permission to explore very far, and exploration metaphysically, creatively, emotionally, and psychologically is exactly what is needed in order for them to heal. They tend to get disillusioned quickly because their mind can be very much like a child's. When things do not go their way they know that they cannot kick and scream, but rather, if they make a ritual of some sort – for example, to perhaps compulsively think or clean – they will feel the release of whatever disappointment they are dealing with in the moment.

There are strong desires of this individual's ego to master the world – that is to say, their own personal world. This one often resists the necessary surrendering of his or her way to inner peace as they have not yet learned this concept and application of Spirit in their lives. The OCD symptoms are present to teach them that to surrender, spiritually speaking, means to win. One is surrendering to their higher self and God so that their world may become put into the best and highest order for them. There is often a tremendous stubbornness in this individual as well as a genuine sweetness. This sweetness is, however, how one learns exactly how to get along with others. It is within this sweetness that others put up with them or understand and have compassion for this part of them, which can be quite annoying to those they know well and love. It is as if others in the life of the one with OCD know on some level how much of an issue of control it is, and in the person's drama they bring them into it as well. Everyone has their own dramas or life situations and conditions to contend with. Therefore, family members can be very much affected on many levels. It is important to recognize, without blaming, that much of one's OCD symptoms can often be learned behavior from parents and/or caregivers. This condition is very much about magical thinking in thinking that one can change their world, but they are merely controlling it, rather than naturally surrendering into the flow of life and Spirit. Of course, one must eventually learn that controlling never works, as "no controlling" is a vital spiritual law.

Evolution on a soul level for these individuals and sometimes for those they love is held up and postponed if this person does not seek and receive help, as well as try to understand and really work with and utilize their condition. One has the right to be understood, yes, but not to be foolish and hurt themselves and/or those they love. If those who love this person with OCD were not so afraid to upset them and were to speak their truth, even though they know they may be "punished" – sometimes harshly – by this one's inner child, things could shift much more quickly and easily for everyone. At times, the person with OCD can make life miserable for others, but they get away with it because of the love that they offer to those they love.

Quite often, those with OCD were overly indulged or, one might say, "spoiled" in some ways as children. They did not grow up as adults in the way of sophistication of Spirit and its world, which now is where this individual's personal work must be focused. It is important for them to be open to and perhaps study all religions as well as the wisdom of the highest spiritual teachers that they can find in the form of books, lectures, or any other important metaphysical material they are guided to. This will aid the soul in its opening and the rapid evolvement necessary to heal themselves.

OCD is so much about controlling oneself, others, events, and situations that a person will often do just about anything to protect their secret, and a secret it often is. It matters not where and when this child developed this syndrome, it only matters that one recognizes that it is really affecting more than themselves in most cases, and that the real lover within them could get help to release their tensions in other ways. Artistically and creatively there are so many ways for this person to be made satisfied, content, and peaceful, as he or she is naturally very artistic and creative. The God within is the Artist within. This person is full of creative energy, although he or she is often unaware of their talent and too afraid to let their wings spread and fly as high as they are quite capable of. A creative and fearless person is who they really are, yet they tend to keep themselves in a safe little box, hiding within the OCD.

Having OCD to different degrees allows one to not have to individuate into their second adulthood, which every human being eventually must. This occurs as one matures spiritually, psychologically, and emotionally and simultaneously evolves into their fullest and most glorious form. A person's conditions and life situations are designed and preprogrammed to speed up this process. If this does not occur in this lifetime, then it will in the next, or the one after that as the Beloved never gives up on its lover, or one could also say, as the Divine never gives up on its child. The OCD is preventing one from the holiest process of Individuation, as this is the process of turning the darkness of one's shadow into the light of the higher self, or from the human self into the Godself. Sensibly speaking, the Individuation process is clearly what is missing in this person's life and is exactly what is now needed most to be focused on in order to heal more quickly and efficiently. The employment or assistance of a Jungian analyst or other spiritualist-type professional whose work with people is largely focused on the work of the inner child and the Individuation process, may be extremely beneficial to a person with OCD, as the inner child is so prevalent and plays such an important role within this condition.

It is important to take into serious consideration that the person who suffers from OCD is in much denial of the happenings of their soul from many lives, not just this one. Without having to explore the lives of the past, often just knowing that this plays a role will help one to let go so they can heal. It is crucial that this person reaches inside and pulls the pain up each and every time they become nervous or anxious and the symptoms of the behavior begin. If he or she would deeply breathe, and say to themselves something like, "Okay, this is an opportunity for me to practice surrender, rather than control. To heal and receive help from my angels, guides, and God, and to once again, surrender my way to inner peace – I will be okay. All is well." In this way, one is learning to soothe themselves properly and manage the emotional body, which is beginning to speak loudly in the form of symptoms. This occurs so that one could have the opportunity to heal a part of their soul and call it back to this time and place where they are safe and all is well. It is important to understand that by them going into obsessive behaviors they could actually, in a very unhealthy way, stop time and the situations at hand. They can stop their own inner world, but it is such a small world, and they can as well then bring others to a halt along with them. If one truly desires to heal and change his or her behavior it is possible. It will also be acceptable to everyone else if they did what they really wanted to do with their life. Often, what this person really desires is not even allowed into their consciousness because just as they begin to feel and hear the real voice of the soul, the ego kicks in and, like a disruptive child, goes into behavior in the way of symptoms. This is the same as giving into the child within, rather than more appropriately and properly parenting themselves, which is what really is being called for each time the OCD behavior begins.

Extreme focus and discipline by these individuals, as well as extreme honesty towards them by those who love and care for them is crucial in the healing of this condition. Those who love them must learn and truly know that part of the higher purpose of the OCD behavior is to teach them that speaking their truth, rather than keeping a false sense of peace, is more important, needed, and necessary for themselves as well as the other to heal. One must take full responsibility for their own healing without blaming another or themselves. One must become one's own best caregiver and healer. Individuals with OCD tend to allow others to unnecessarily parent them. This is most unhealthy to the psyche of everyone involved, not just the one with this condition. The person with OCD has a great opportunity now to learn how to joyfully parent themselves in the most amazing and creative ways. There are many gifts in disguise for this person and all those that they share this life with, but it is up to the bravery of this individual to ask to have their gifts revealed, cultivated, and shared. ✘

PANIC DISORDER

Learning How to Listen to the Spirit
The Awakening, Recognition, and Utilization of One's Spiritual Gifts

Panic disorder comes from the part of the brain that was left over before and after birth. There was a part of the brain that had yet to be filled in order for the remembrance of the soul to be born into full form. People who experience panic disorder are those who are an extremely sensitive type. They are often considerably psychic, yet they were often raised with much fear and criticism of such gifts. These gifts are often located in the deep walls and energy system of the psyche of the parents of children who suffer from panic disorder. The parent's gifts were never really and truly fully developed, so the child is raised without any knowledge, reassurance, or nurturance, of their own empathic abilities. They are raised much more so to be realistic and "in the brain" rather than heart. The parents did not develop their own psychic gifts; therefore, the child cannot develop theirs until later in life.

There is often quite a bit of parental resentment, especially with the mother of children with panic disorder. They resent on a deep level that they were never mirrored in the way that they needed to be in order to develop their gifts, so they often end up in professions to please someone other than themselves, such as a parent or spouse. These individuals also often go into professions where they *think* they should be and focus more on making a living, rather than making a life. Those who suffer from panic attacks are often natural healers and are in a deeper need of going into the healing profession, yet most often choose something much more mainstream and in the "public eye", so to speak.

These individuals are in need of exclusivity and reclusiveness in order to develop their spiritual gifts that are often extremely underdeveloped. Thankfully, their spirit gives them panic so that they do not miss their mark in following their destiny. This one tends to need things in a big way, thus panic attacks are created. Even the name panic attack is grand in tone and feeling and suggests one is being attacked. Although there are often many physical characteristics present during a panic attack, this is an illusion and proves the power of the mind of these individuals in that they could create such amazing symptoms. These symptoms come so incredibly harsh and crash at times because it is exactly what will lead them to seek necessary emotional and psychological as well as physical help. What they most often are leaving out, however, is spiritual healing, which is what they are in most need of. This is because the root cause of panic disorder is that the spirit is not being listened to and must be. The only thing to get the attention of these individuals is such an *attack* of Spirit. Spiritual gifts must be born in everyone, but especially those with panic disorder. They are in critical need of attaining spiritual healing and understanding of their own psyche. They have so much to offer yet cannot utilize their gifts and are unaware that this is the root cause and effect of panic. This person tends to be very profound on the level of the soul and they have a profound like condition reflecting this aspect of them.

When this child or adult is brought (which they will many times in their life) right to Spirit's door, with a connection of some sort offering help, it is often refused. The healer or teacher offering assistance gracefully then goes on their way. There will, however, always be another opportunity for this soul. Eventually they will learn to live a very synchronistic lifestyle. To live comfortably, one with panic disorder must loosen his or her hold on society and the way they think it and they should be. Where they should live, what profession they should have, and even questions such as how many children they should have, are all matters that separate them from their intuition. Rather than being open to the highest good of all, too much control is often issued by these individuals. Trying to control can create panic in just about anyone, but especially those who are very sensitive and live with this condition. A very important law of the Universe is to learn to not control people, situations, events, etc., and eventually everyone must learn this law, as this is law itself.

When people with panic disorder go into places where many psyches are roaming around they can become very disturbed and panic will often set in. These individuals must learn how to know the difference as to what is coming from them and what is coming from another. They often merge their energy unhealthily with those that they love, and those that they are yet to know. The individual who panics is most often one who is a very old soul who has seen much heartache in lives gone by. Part of the panic of this lifetime is the remembrance and the bringing of the past, present, and future into the *now space,* where they are struggling to live in the moment. The most important thing for these people to do is to repeatedly check in with themselves about how they are feeling and see if they are in the present moment or another, especially the future of their lives. If it is even five minutes from where they are, it is too far away from the moment. To be truly in the moment is to know all is well, and always was, and always will be. Remember, to be in the *now* is to be in the *know.*

Excellent healing modalities for those who suffer with panic disorder are biofeedback, deep conscious breathing, yoga, relaxation, movie watching, or book reading where higher consciousness topics are expressed, discussed, and/or taught. Those who experience panic attacks are generally very good at absorbing information and both positive and negative vibrations. Therefore, one must always work on being focused, conscious, and aware as to what, where, when, why, and how they are energetically consuming. It is especially helpful to see where and when one is energetically consuming their environment and everyone in it. Staying in positive energy a good part of the day is essential for healing and reconstruction of the soul. One must consciously choose positive atmospheres in which to re-raise themselves utilizing their spiritual gifts and teaching them to others as they graciously and spontaneously are learning to move throughout their day.

PARKINSON'S

Learning How to Create Peace for Oneself
Tremendous Opportunity for Spiritual Growth
and Evolution of the Soul

Parkinson's occurs in individuals who are a long time in coming to their spiritual nature. They do not, however, honor this part of themselves more than they honor other outside appearances in the ways of the ego, such as making money and relationships with others, rather than themselves and their spirit. These individuals often live their lives in an almost secret misery about something that they just cannot put their hands on. They are not sure that they are doing what they would really like to be doing, so they are often on a search for something to do that is better than the life they have created for themselves.

Parkinson's occurs so that partners, if there is one, can become truly the best friend of the other. Often, these two butt heads quite a bit in the way the world is, and the way their inner worlds, and personal worlds, are as well. Often the intimate relationships in their lives, usually the most intimate, are the ones that are quite strained, and the work is not done to make them connect in the way the spirit of both is desired. Usually, the one with Parkinson's is so involved in his own life and affairs that he does not pay much attention to those he loves. He then creates a very busy life of his own so he does not have to deal with matters of the heart and soul. These issues become so buried in the body, brain, and often heart, that the Parkinson's manifests to help one reject things in their lives that are not as important as family matters. These individuals tend to have had a hard time committing to the life of family and often relate more to friends. This is simply because there are issues of forgiveness that must come to fruition in the way that one must forgive those that they love, or that have loved them the most, but did not have the expression of that love in the form of the physical.

These individuals as children were often extremely lonely, sometimes depressed, and lived in a life full of fantasy within their own minds. Often, few and sometimes not even one person could or would validate their souls. These children were, and as adults are, of very high mind, but it is not one that many understand and they are thought of by some as very selfish and self-centered. However, it is not so much that they are those things, as they are visionaries who have not had the fertile ground in which to grow in this lifetime. They are often successful in their careers; however a doom and gloom can sometimes lie beyond their outside personalities, and this can be extremely confusing and frustrating to those around him. This person needs much in the support of presence when he is being spoken to. Something triggers in these souls and they go into symptoms, ticks, and distracted frustrations when they feel they are not being seen and heard for who they really are. They get so sad and almost scared on the level of their psyche when they do not get what they need from others, but they do not know that this is what is wrong. They do not know what they truly desire. Often, affection is desired. They are not, however, the most affectionate and are often preoccupied. The Parkinson's comes calling to get them to go deep inside, and also to show others they need something in the way of attention, and they get it with the symptoms. The symptoms are saying, *Here look at me! Do you see I am not at peace? I am suffering – do something for me*. But, what they must learn is that they did not learn to do this for themselves. They did not learn to create peace for themselves, so they rely on others to give it to them. Those around them simply cannot, as their spirits will not allow this because this person really needs and desires to learn how to create peace for himself.

The symptoms mirror this person's deep frustration in the way of wanting to make their mark in this world, so they make symptoms, rather than create the dreams of their soul. They tend to think of these dreams as being somewhat silly. They do not take time to explore their fantasies and dreams on a very large and child-like exploration. Since it is in the imagination in which we heal, as our passions are then revealed, it is this that this person needs most to spiritually heal himself. It is his birthright to be spiritually sound and healed and in complete control of his emotional, physical, and mental self, but this person does not believe in himself on a soul level. He does not think enough about his soul's mission and where he truly could be of most service in the way of what he does, not only for a living, but during his day-to-day life as well.

The deep frustration felt by these individuals reflects a time in their lives when they felt very alone and frustrated. They could greatly benefit by journaling their feelings but, putting pen to paper is a task most of these individuals generally do not do, nor do they think it will help. However, this person must start to do things he would not normally think or agree to do, as this is what his spirit is calling for: to try new things that will get him in touch with his Divine feminine side, which everyone has, but often lies in deep disguise. This is especially the case with these individuals and this opening can make an enormous difference in their lives. This can be a very exciting time because if this person seeks spiritual treatment in any form he can imagine, or take advice from someone who lives and breathes from these higher realms, he will find himself embarking on some great opportunities to get things done for himself and for the world on a much larger scale.

People who suffer with this condition are quite often those of very high mind who have so much to offer others in the way of wisdom and knowledge about scientific things, whether they are conscious of this or not. They are, or can become, very intrigued with how the human mind works and the management of that. There is a great inner desire to tap as deeply as they possibly can into this. To study metaphysics in this lifetime, and at this time in their lives, is something that would help aid them to not only discover their highest self, but also their highest mission and attainment of personal spiritual healing. Parkinson's is something that can offer one extreme pressure as well as extreme pleasure if one is open to new ideas, therapies, and medicine. There is nothing that can help those who are in much pain, and/or frustration and fear, as any type of focused and conscious spiritual growth opportunities. This person can be helped tremendously by seeking out mystics and the reading of sacred texts as well as ancient mystical poetry. The "big guns", so to speak, are often needed to blast open the heart of this person and when that happens, healing is free to occur within the soul and the spirit can be set free as it was designed and born to be.

PELVIC PAIN

The Birthing of One's Own Spirit and Its Ideas
Time to Explore New Realms and Bring Out
the Wild Divine One Within

The pelvic region represents a great deal to women and pain experienced in this area is a common complaint, as they are *dying* to give birth to their spirituality. Along with this spiritual birth comes the revealing of one's true identity, which is the Godself, and along with this comes revealing one's true feelings, including one's spiritual insecurities.

Unexplained pelvic pain comes from much withheld resentment, as well as punishment of the self for the crimes of others. Women experiencing this condition are trying to heal, but doing so from a much *younger* healer and teacher than they are actually capable of being and have been born to become. This is a time when the pelvis is in a flare-up of sorts and these women are discovering how and truly desire to transmute the pain of others for the sake of the world without causing pain and/or sacrifice to themselves.

Metaphysically speaking, the pelvis is about long-standing owing to the Universe what was promised by this woman to *deliver*; yet she remains afraid of what the world especially friends, peers, and coworkers may think of her. As well, if she has a partner this is also playing a significant role in her condition. It is within the relationship with the self that all others will evolve and grow on a spiritual level, which is what the pelvic pain is *crying* out for. This woman's true and higher purpose cannot be birthed, so her pelvis feels the pain of a birth that's true time has not yet come. She feels late in birthing *her* time in the Universe, which must not be taken lightly. Incongruently, she feels unworthy or truly deserving of her plans to go into action, as she is often the caretaker of other's plans. And, although subtle, this does get into her realm of consciousness. She is one for doing too much for others and not receiving enough in return. She must now realize that the Universe often pays one back in ways much more glorious than that of others. This is especially true when one is involved intimately with the ego of others, which in this case can be quite often. Too frequently she is dealing on the level of the ego with others, rather than the soul, which is where the majority of her pain is coming from. In reality, the pain is her unexpressed frustration from the higher self. Her body is *acting out,* rather than expressing herself from the heart.

There is also fear left inside of this woman from long ago, which she now is giving birth to as she experiences the mysterious or rather mystical pain. This is the letting go of the fears of her past, as well as the fears she has taken on for the race of the human. This soul is often one for "losing control" in a very positive and wild way. However, the *wild divine one within* is still too suppressed. She therefore creates pain and turmoil so as to feel the *fire* in some way, but there are much more pleasant ways of doing this. Dancing, breathwork, and/or yoga can each individually or combined be very successful in the self-healing of this condition. Much of the condition of unexplained pelvic pain, as well as many other conditions, is coming from one's unexpressed passion and joy. This woman's *spiritual juice* or energy, which is the *liquid light* of the Divine, must be released. If one does not find appropriate ways for this light to be liquidated they will create pain of some type in its place.

Pelvic pain where there is no medical explanation or cure must be looked at with a fine-toothed comb. This condition is all about the self and its selfless acts secretly waiting to be acknowledged and rewarded. The higher self, however, desires no credit for its actions and waits only for the *little self* to catch up to it. In the meantime, the pain can often be increased, but can just as easily disappear if one looks to follow the voice within itself. One must listen carefully to the pain in order to decode it. One must ask it, *Why are you here? What are you trying to ask or tell me and causing me so much pain because I am not listening to you and intuiting you clearly and as impeccably as only I can do?*

You are looking to find value in and of yourself, rather than through the eyes or voice of another. You are learning your own self-worth and decoding your secret mission, the one that only *you* can give birth to. There are always many *contractions of love* in giving birth to the self, and a very important part of a person's spiritual journey is learning how to make oneself as comfortable as possible during the contractions involved in birthing the *Divine self*. Metaphysically speaking, this is an exciting time, as healing is being birthed and with healing always comes opening and evolution of the soul. There will always be growing pains as one stretches to reach up to the level of the higher self, which is the Godself within and without.

Women experiencing this condition are learning patience for their fellow human beings. They are learning to not actually do or heal through feeling the pain of others, but rather to help people to transmute and heal themselves by birthing their *own* spirit and its ideas. They are also learning to make the decisions necessary in their life in the way of the care and feeding of their own souls. These women are learning to discipline themselves in the most necessary routine possible for their greatest good. No one but themselves can do this for them. They have secretly been giving to others what they themselves have craved for others to do for them. They are now learning (as everyone eventually must) the spiritual lesson and truth that no one can heal you but you.

If you have been experiencing pelvic pain, now is the time in your life to explore new realms and do anything you can imagine to bring out the goddess within, the sensual playful one, as this *wild divine one* knows that often the best way is to play, which now is deeply craved. Joy and peace rather than sorrow and pain are looking to be the better part of the day. Expanding and powerfully exploding into the rest of your time on the Earth plane is occurring. You are now in the process of lightening your load and setting a more appropriate tone for who you really are for the rest of your life. You must now *only* claim your treasure held within. It is not only meant for you to discover this treasure shrouded in pain, it is your Divine Right to do so. Go and dive into your own well and discover all the mouthwatering treats you have been baking within your own soul and that of the Beloved's. The time has come for you to align your wills as one.

PLANTAR FASCIITIS – FOOT CONDITIONS

Learning to Lighten Up, Be Playful, and Eliminate Judgment
A Time to Listen More to the Voice of the Soul and
Make Conscious Connection to the Divine

The first thing an individual suffering from plantar fasciitis must do is to ask themselves, *Are my feet actually on the ground, or am I putting myself into a race to get to the Divine within?* If this is the case, these individuals must now truly know that this is a lifelong process, meant to be enjoyed, and the little moments are meant to be relished. Discomfort in the feet is present to get these individuals to pay attention to the playful spirit that is within them.

Those with this condition tend to become *bound* with their own rigidness. The type of thing that tends to irritate them is often the smallest of matters. They are now learning not to judge. Often they judge, but do not realize this because they are in denial about this part of the shadow, which is actually in constant irritation and judgment of themselves or others. Plantar fasciitis is about uncontrolled and unacknowledged judgment, as well as rigidity in thinking. A person with this condition must work to keep an open mind in all areas of life, and as well to always remind themselves of this tendency to judge. It is the unconscious part of the shadow that creates the symptoms so they can finally be revealed and then healed. They can then move on in life and be freed to do more playful and fun things. These individuals often take life too seriously, as well as their part in the big picture. Constantly remembering to lighten up and laugh at themselves whenever they can rather than judge is a very good remedy for this condition.

These individuals are learning to "love thyself". Their soul, the child within, is seeking some tender loving care from themselves, not necessarily to receive from anyone else. A person with these symptoms must pray and ask themselves, *Why do my heels or feet hurt? What is this about?* And, *Why are you here?* Then journal and/ or meditate about why this condition has come into your life. *Why are you calling through my feet and heels and what is it that I desire most in this or any moment?*

This condition is an opportunity for much growth and connection to the Divine. Use it and don't waste time. Stop, ask, and listen to your higher self. Let it answer you with love, and freedom, and insights, rather than scream for your attention in the way of painful symptoms. Eventually, we must all get to what we really need and desire from deep inside our souls. This is the only reason we suffer – to get us closer to the effects of having the Divine a constant and present force in our lives. These and all symptoms are clues in disguise waiting for you to take yourself and your purpose of loving and caring for yourself seriously so that your soul can ultimately fly free with ease.

This condition is here to motivate you to go within and learn about yourself. This is true of any problem or concern, but plantar fasciitis in particular is very much about learning how to care for oneself in new, but *old* ways, such as meditation, prayer, writing, and bathing. Absolutely anything that brings gentleness and calmness into your life you must look to do and thoroughly allow yourself to enjoy. The *loving oneself into ecstasy* is what will heal any pain of body, mind, and/or spirit. To be able to connect oneself with the Godself and make this the number one job in life is

112

what wants to become your main lifestyle. This is the most important work in your life right now. You *are* your job and you *are* your purpose first and foremost! You are learning to put yourself and your love for you first. It is only in this way that you can be of highest service to anyone else. You know this intellectually, but it must be known and felt on the level of the heart and soul as well. The soul cannot and will not be fooled.

Plantar fasciitis can be a very painful condition and one who holds on tightly to the idea of a very "spoiled child" is the one who will suffer most with the symptoms. One must ask themselves, *Where am I spoiling things for myself or another that I truly love, but tend to make things difficult for them by moaning and complaining about certain things in life that are actually quite easy to rectify?* This person tends to look to another in the way of complaining or acting out emotionally with tears and/or anger so that someone else will heal their pain. But the truth is only they can truly heal themselves.

This individual must learn to stop and listen to the voice of the soul the moment they find themselves going to someone else for the answers they have within. These individuals tend to be lazy and lack the discipline needed on a daily basis in order to connect with the Divine within. Those with plantar fasciitis tend to think as well that others' connection to the Divine for them is closer than their own, which is, of course completely untrue. No one truly knows you better than you know yourself. Once this person gets the hang of being there for themselves above all else they will soon discover most of what they have been concerned about is simply illusion, and what so desperately wishes to be reborn, renewed and refreshed is their most holy God-given connection to the Source from which it was created.

PLEOMORPHIC ADENOMA TUMOR

A Great Teacher of Patience and Spirit
Opportunity to Gain New Information and Learn
to Live Consciously In The Moment

The condition called Pleomorphic Adenoma comes from living in very underdeveloped levels of intelligence, so a tumor of such nature will grow to activate one's greatest mission. These individuals need to study and learn to fill the spaces in their minds that can occupy so much. The tumor will grow if the space is not filled appropriately. These individuals are of high intelligence, especially in the area of science and metabolism. Also, they can grasp more easily than most any subject that could be considered strange to most, or very new thought topics. People with this type of tumor are always on a quest spiritually for something new in the way of knowledge and this often is not yet explored, and therefore, a tumor can grow in its place.

There is a lack of separation and temptation in these individuals. They must separate more from those that they love and they must stop imparting their will upon them. This type of tumor, as with all tumors, grows to fight off the infection of one's personality characteristics that can impart not only their will upon another, but also on those they have yet to meet, which is actually a much more appropriate place to put their intelligence upon rather than those closest to their hearts. Family members will often struggle with the strengths of these individuals and this is to teach them to let go and move on to where there is an open door rather than stay stuck at a closed one. This is only a temporary condition of those closest to them and it is there so that they simply find a larger, more appropriate audience. These individuals often lack the temptation to find their own way, which is difficult for them because it is often quite out of the average box. Their path is not an ordinary one and the tumor becomes one's friend in the end because it is often the catalyst to let them out of the box. These individuals can sometimes really box themselves into uncomfortable situations, which creates a lot of frustration and can steer them to leading more of a life outside of reality. They can live in a state of denial of certain characteristics in their personalities, and this also must be explored.

Those who develop this condition are of highly underdeveloped intention as well as intelligence. They spend much of their time worrying about others and the habits of others rather than about themselves, which is what this type of tumor is there to teach them. The pleomorphic adenoma is there to teach one to look more closely in the mirror of themselves. This means to go deep in the eyes of everyone they find themselves in contact with - see yourself and others more clearly. Don't postpone things until tomorrow. The message with this condition is to live in the moment and as consciously as you can. This is the primary lesson you are learning. When the tumor goes away one will never be the same, as it is almost as though they have had a near death experience without the danger of death. The seed is planted with the tumor's birth of one's destiny and mission. This condition offers much in the way of abandonment of one's ill wishes and births the wishes and the dreams of the soul. With the loss of the tumor goes the loss of the ego.

These individuals have to learn the power of the heart, mind, and soul to heal any situation much more than that of the physical. These individuals are interested on a very deep level about the whole of community. The whole of the Universe and their soul mission is about anything having to do with the oneness of all – universally speaking, the oneness of the all in the entire Universe, not just that of the world in which they live. These individuals have a natural connection and openness, once discovered, to that of any life elsewhere of any type. There is special extraterrestrial-type energy with all those who carry this type of signature of pleomorphic adenoma. It is very interesting to study these individuals. If they met others with the same condition they would feel as though they were meeting soul family.

These individuals realize that one must put themselves out into the world, yet they have a strong fear of being taken away from the ones they love. Again, it is important that they realize they can tend to try to control and often intimidate those they love as well. They are not quite conscious of the intimidation component, but they are conscious of their controlling of others. They have a sweetness to them and a real caring, but it can be quite overbearing to those they love.

These individuals can be helped if they look very deeply within. They are those that must do the study of themselves and leave absolutely nothing out. It is crucial that they do their inner work of both child and adult. They are stuck in some time when they were young and the denial or normalization of this time in their lives is what is rolled up in a safe, nice little ball within themselves so that they can one day, in one big shot, let it go.

Surgery is strongly suggested to relieve this situation because it is about issues so deeply stored in the unconscious that one may have to have help to remove it completely. The very good news is that if one is conscious of this, when one has the surgery they will know for sure that when they wake and recuperate a bit that they will have grown in spiritual maturity by leaps and bounds in the time it takes to get better and be back on their feet. There is a huge energetic relief of negative emotions when the tumor is removed. There is a lift and a great rise in the vibration of the holder of the tumor. It is barren fruit and must be removed or dissolved once it has run its usefulness. Once the tumor is removed there is much room made for all the new information that these individuals are craving on a very important and deep level.

Personal relationships are taken to degrees beyond human comprehension with these individuals, so a lot of their energy is wasted in the wrong place. They function best in large crowds with like-minded individuals. They also strongly dislike to be kept waiting on any level and become easily frustrated with the unconscious behavior of others. This tumor, as with all types of tumors, is greatly intended to be utilized as a teacher of Spirit and patience. These individuals are now learning the importance and the magnitude of their personal creation. They are also learning how to now, especially, become their own best of healers, as they solidify more deeply their own connection to the Divine and its mind.

PREMATURE EJACULATION

Opportunity for Spiritual, Emotional, and Sexual Advancement
Learning to Create Stimulation, Togetherness, and Closeness

Premature Ejaculation is a condition that comes from deep sexual insecurities, as well as those times that were troubled as one was growing up and what he saw or perceived intimate relationships to be. These individuals get stuck in a time when they were or are quite nearsighted in their judgment. They tend to be very critical thinkers in a positive way, but that criticism also comes in a negative way that is most often directed at their partner. These individuals tend to not be able to be very open with their feelings and in order to have good and satisfying sexual relationships one must be willing to process their deepest feelings. There is much frustration held deeply within this person. He is often one who looks at the glass half empty, rather than full, although he often thinks highly of himself and feels that he is a rather positive person. The truth is, however, that this one is "one of a kind" in the areas of kindness and politeness, but also there is a certain phoniness to him, which his partner notices and cannot seem to completely shake their negative feelings towards him, which only adds to his condition, which therefore is a condition of both.

This is so frustrating that the partner often closes the door out of fear of failure of the relationship, but the truth is they must open the door again, as the energy of fear continues to build and this gets worse with time and age, as this one already believes that he is getting old much too quickly for his liking. This fear is a direct reflection of his fear that he better hurry up and "get it while he can" because he may not be here too much longer. Rather than being the type who stops to smell the roses, the person who suffers with premature ejaculation rushes though life and often leads his professional and personal lives on a schedule with much pressure upon it, which penetrates his psyche and then penetrates his penis and performance. He is actually in a rush as well to get to the *other side* in the way of orgasm because this is when he is in the most holy space. This individual tends to live far away from his spirit and its knowing. This is a very difficult aspect of his personality, which makes it difficult to live with him. This is especially the case if his partner is of unique spiritual nature. Sex becomes a thing of the past, but it always lies in the *present* of the relationship, and therefore must be discussed and worked on if there is ever to be deep peace in the relationship. One must never blame the other, which often, out of fear, judgment, and disillusionment of life, becomes the difficult case.

The time must come when this person settles into a quiet routine and when he focuses consciously on trimming his life and its activities and does anything at all that he finds relaxing and practices this regularly. Each and every day is a day for healing for him, but he is often resistant to this part of his world. He thinks most often that he is fine and everyone else *is* not. This again is where he stands in judgment and can then explore the greatest realms as well. He tends to believe his own illusions of separateness between people so he puts himself in a false higher place yet believes it to be a heaven space. He is often quite a paradox in the making or he is already formed as such.

This person is a very deep thinker and has immense potential in the psychic realms, which therefore means he can derive much pleasure out of sex. However, he still refuses this part of his nature and therefore his most primal and spiritual nature as well will suffer. Since he lives on the surface much of the day, or at least tries very hard to keep himself busy so that he has no time to go deep within himself, his partner, or any other, unless things become so painful he has no choice. Then comes the real difficult time because if one is very intimate with this person in the way of closeness of family, friendship, or partnership, he finds it difficult and almost annoying that he has to be bothered into being connected and open on a deeper level. Yet, this is exactly what is needed for this condition to improve. This man tends to secretly blame his partner for difficulties in his own personality to make him feel better about himself. This creates a distasteful cycle between lovers, so much so that the partner then eventually can refuse to be intimate at all for they feel completely alone. This is most unhealthy for the partner as well, which is why this is a condition shared by both in the relationship. The partner too must grow and go deep within to explore what it is that *they* truly desire and are silently demanding with their frustration and/ or disgust with the situation. The condition has been created to actually bring or ultimately bring the couple stimulation, togetherness, and closeness that was never really present before. However, these gifts lie dormant waiting to be discovered and fully enjoyed. The individuals involved are each stubborn and in need of spiritual and sexual healing. This can be done together or apart, meaning on their own in their own time. However, something must be done and that must be agreed upon by the individuals.

Pressure builds up and creates a worse situation and that is what makes it so unbearable. The couple can give up and lose a wonderful and healing part of themselves individually, as well as a couple. The relationship here is one of silent suffering most often and when this occurs and is recognized healing can begin and not a moment before. This is something that has to rise and shine and come out into the open for discussion of many things, not just sexual things. The research and practice of tantra is essential and a great aid to improving this situation. When one heals a bit of themselves they automatically heal a bit of their partner. It is often the deepest desire of both parties that they remain close emotionally, physically, and spiritually and there is no better way to accomplish this than sexually and with the practice of sacred sexuality.

There are also the areas of boredom and unhappiness that must be explored with this condition, as well as discussing the disappointments about themselves and the other, as well as others, including the parents of the couple because often they had much to do with this as these children's parents most often had unusual sexual relations, if much of any at all. So much of this condition is a learned part, as when one is older one is not fed romantically enough, or emotionally or spiritually enough, and all this is the world in which sex is formed and used for creation. Therefore, this cannot be left out or ignored. This is very sad for anyone involved. The deepest of communication is what is most desired and needed by this couple, and if one is on their own and not in a couple relationship all this still applies. This one must find someone that they trust to talk to about their feelings and all else presented on this topic.

If strong and meaningful initiative is taken to improve this most important area in one's life, the rewards of joy, health, companionship, tenderness, and togetherness will naturally begin to flow at a very normal, regular, and satisfying rate. But one must first set their intention of what and why they desire this and begin to pay attention more deeply as to how they are feeling about this part of their life as well as their partner. This condition can truly become the highlight and greatest gift bringer of your entire lives.

PREMENSTRUAL TENSION SYNDROME (PMS)

A Time for a Woman's Spirit to Receive More Attention, Direction,
and Territory in order to Utilize Her Gifts
Learning to Live Life in Accordance to the Higher Self

The problem with understanding the symptomatic temporary condition called PMS is that it is a condition that is one where many people can become the target for the aggression of the self that is held within. A woman becomes tense and irritated at the things other people are doing, but they are a reflection of at least a sliver of her own sheltered and shielded ego. This woman becomes weepy, irritated, angry, depressed, etc. – all the feelings that are now coming up during this time to heal. Metaphorically speaking, it comes at this time to a point of boiling water, yet there is no pasta in the water. Meaning that in the condition of PMS the individual is fully ready to cook something – to "cook up" a part of her new life that is trying to emerge. During the more normal part of her cycle she is content to live a life that is more regular, but during the symptomatic time the spirit is screaming for more attention, more direction, and more territory to utilize her gifts. This is the time her

122

frustrations emerge, but what is emerging is confused. What is emerging is actually her desire to serve not destroy.

PMS does destroy the part of the ego that is so deep in hiding that it needs to be shown in such an extreme way. The frustrations in this woman are something that those around her are actually (although often unconsciously) afraid of her healing. These frustrations, however, are the parts of her shadow that need to be revealed. She is often suppressed and unsupported by those on her path on a daily level. By the time her period comes near she can no longer *act* as if there is nothing bothering her and the PMS symptoms emerge to let the negative feelings go so that she does not become ill. PMS headaches are a perfect example of this. All comes to the surface to release what is no longer necessary and no longer serves the soul. Hormones are playing a necessary part, but they would not need to become out of balance if this individual worked diligently all month in preparation for what is in reality her *time of power,* which is going to try once again to emerge this month and make a shift so radical in her consciousness that she actually heals this part of her shadow that is coming up to heal.

The time before a woman's period and during the beginning of it she is one who is usually so tired of being someone else, and serving those who serve her not, that she takes issue or fit with everyone around her, unless it is someone who is truly of an unconditionally loving space, which is often not at all too familiar in this person's life. She is, through PMS symptoms, trying to relieve the pain she experiences from feeling unconnected to the Divine in herself and others.

PMS is, in fact, very easily cured if one will take the "bull within" by the horns and speak gently and lovingly to her. No one else can really ever give her all of what she is learning to give to herself in the way of comfort and ease. She often looks too much to please others who really are not interested in the pleasure or pleasures of her. Her hormones literally are moaning out her grief and disbelief of the part of her life that she has not only created but also perpetuated. She is often one to act silly and then stop herself as if to blame herself for not being serious enough, but this one is in fact one who needs to, especially at this time, play and act silly all throughout her day. It is within this playfulness that her tensions will release in the way of proper functioning and communicating. This time of PMS is a time when one's spirit is saying, *Please, I am begging you to look at me – look in my eyes and see me for all of who I am. Even though I am not seen by you – I see you all too clearly for how magnificent you are.*

The symptoms of PMS are teaching a woman and the men around her, as well as children, coworkers, etc., that she is worthy of not only love but the true impressions that she leaves upon the hearts of others. This woman does not truly accelerate her own spirit for fear that she will hold the spirit of another's back or make others in some way uncomfortable. The PMS condition will thankfully repeat itself and very easily could compete with itself to make the symptoms progressively worse so that she will finally live in accordance to the higher self of her own and no one else's.

PMS is a time in a woman's life that is crucial for being self-examined and initiated into her womanhood – her true womanhood – over and over again. Each month she has to have the time to be quiet and reflective so as to align herself with her highest self. When she sees herself getting excited and angry or passionate about something, which is most often really the case, her passions are trying to come out, but they are in such disguise that they cannot be *read* by her or others involved in her life. But if she gives herself space and time each month to go deeply within she will see how she is angry at only herself for being in the space of where grace cannot live or breathe. The Divine within is *cramped up* in pain of symptoms and is begging for relief. This woman is begging to be seen for the beauty and queen she has yet to fully reveal for fear of loss of complete ego-self. The symptoms of PMS are a very necessary part of a woman's realization of her highest dreams and mission. When she relaxes into the blooms that which she radiates she will fall into the very polished star that she was born to give shine to. She will then become the lover in full form she was destined to become.

PSORIASIS

Learning to Touch and Heal as a Servant of the Divine
Calming the Body Down With One's Own Hands
Bringing Intelligence and Wisdom to Consciousness
and Sharing It with Others

The problem with those suffering with psoriasis is something coming more from within than without (including relationship and/or environmental issues). This condition stems from the residue of a painful past for this soul – painful memories that this person does not wish to face for fear they may not be the good person they strongly desire to be. These memories within the soul, however, are not necessarily this one's responsibility to heal, as others who have mistreated them in the past have caused them. Psoriasis forms similar to layers of pain and stored up blood and must release itself from the soul's wounding while in recovery of the past, which can include the pasts of previous incarnations. Those who contract this condition of the skin and tissues within are old souls who often times are in a state of *hearing* the call of the wounded, as they can relate well to their own call of the past.

125

How can one relieve and rid themselves of this condition? First of all this is not something you want to rid yourself of as it is something one can attribute most of life's battle wounds, put them in a jar once and for all, and as they flake off the body with each flare-up of sorts, much intelligence and wisdom of the ages is brought to this person's consciousness. The only way this comes is in the form of the rash-type feeling and substance.

Individuals with psoriasis must consider and explore some thing(s) of significance that are bothering or deeply upsetting them. Generally, however, they are not ones for making trouble where they feel it unnecessary to do so and /or that it may bring trouble upon their own painful past. Psoriasis is difficult to heal, as one is often in an agitated state when in a flare-up, while they actually need to be as calm as possible. They must be alone and calm in a state rather of creativity and charm. This *charismatic charm* comes from within. If one is not utilizing their charm with others, they will, in fact, create the charm in the form of a body disorder. Something is *itching* its way out of this person, but the soul is not yet conscious of the best way to rebirth itself into a much fuller version of themselves – a fuller form, if you will.

Psoriasis is not an easy thing to carry as it can easily spread if focused upon. As well, the issue(s) with this condition can be cured with the mind more easily than most disorders. This person now has the opportunity to learn deep healing techniques. His or her abilities are trying to be born; however, they do not go deeply enough into their own psyche, which is always being called for when feeling symptoms. There is also the truth to be considered and explored about whatever this person is currently finding unattractive about him or herself. They must now work harder on whatever issue(s) there are, whether having to do with the body, mind, sense of style, or simply themselves and their life in general.

When in a flare-up, quite often this person wants to retreat, but this is when they must seek to go outside into the world and offer their gifts, as the world waits for them to grace it with their presence. There is a part of them, the most important part, that they are trying to mask and escape or get away without talking about or sharing their wisdom. They are learning to be afraid of people at this time in their lives and so become almost untouchable to others unconsciously. This occurs because they feel somewhat guilty about taking pleasure with being alone and completely on their own, which is a great hidden desire for those with this condition. In fact, they need this alone time very much, but at the same time they are afraid of this.

As long as these individuals are taking extreme care of themselves they will heal the problem they are experiencing with their skin. The skin is an organ that holds the *garbage* or *trash* of the Universe within it. It is like a shell over the body and forces one to not have the "patience of a saint", so to speak, which often times is the case with many of those with this condition. The truth, however, is that this person now is intentionally having to lose their own space, as well as their patience. The space one is losing is the space they now have just for them. There is a time for being alone and creating and there is a time for sharing the creation. *You* are the creation, and you are meant to be shared and heard in the way that only you can be heard.

Your heart is also in a triangle of sorts with some others in your life and you must come to terms with how you truly feel about those you love, without guilt or any strings attached. Your body is telling you how you feel and that is sore and irritated, as well as confused as to why you have manifested the condition. If you ask yourself why have you brought this on and remain open to see what the answer might be, if answered quite honestly it will most likely be that you hear something such as this, *I do not want to do this anymore. I want to have fun and I want to explore. I want to experience the joy I know I have touched before, but this time it is going to be in a huge way and it is going to be fun.* The ego says, *Oh no! I am going to create a rash to fight you to stay in misery with me."*

The soul wants to go home and bring that *home* back to the earth while sleeping, and then too while awake. However, the problem for this person is that they are too young on a soul level to let others down so they worry too much about the cause and effect of things, rather than living and working spontaneously enough. This soul is free, but imprisons him or herself and then blames others for not getting out and about on the level of where they could be and where they know they can fly. This causes the irritation and pain. It is but not being able to sing and dance with others, so this one stays alone trapped in their own mind and body. The skin says, *Let me out!* It cries to let it free, but the ego is the little self that says, *No, what about me!* And, *If I am alone, so too are you, so there!* This is a very child-like position this person is in during this part of their life. This one is much older intellectually, but shares not enough of their wisdom; therefore, a rash is created so that they deal with what needs to be dealt with so as to free themselves to not be afraid to heal and love without conditions.

This is a time when this individual requires total and deep communication and reflection about their life so they may create a serious plan of action. It is also time for this one to learn how to calm their body down with their own hands. This person is a hands on healer who needs to touch and be touched, and if not, forms unattractive markings that say to others the opposite of what is truly desired. Psoriasis says, *Do not touch me because I am not worthy.* This comes from lifetimes of having skin disorders where they were taken from their community because of how they looked and/or out of fear that they could or would hurt others. It is important to remember that this is partially a condition of the past, which has bled into this life. This person needs to touch and be touched so they can heal this other lifetime(s), as well as the present.

Too much medication will mask the symptoms of the psyche, which must turn into gold, for that is what is written in the horoscope of this soul. One must touch as a servant of the Divine that they are. There is no reason to worry about anything. All is well and as it should be. The condition of psoriasis is telling you that *you* are anything but irritated or irritating. This is what you must understand and believe first beyond a shadow of your doubt. This is part of the Divine alchemy of humankind and a wonderful example as to how individual experiences and conditions are used as the chemicals to turn one back into the gold they were made from. ⚥

128

RHEUMATOID ARTHRITIS

Opportunity to Keep Up with the Passions of One's Spirit
Learning to Let Go of the Old, Try New Things,
and Encourage Self and Others

Rheumatoid arthritis strikes those who are extremely rigid and stubborn in their thinking. This condition can be very painful and causes one to attract much needed attention to themselves. Whether negative or positive attention this one does not care, as they are often loved-starved individuals. They are generally very needy, but act as though they are not wanting to trouble anyone around them. They are those who feel deserving of a good time, but feel they have been dealt a bad hand and often feel sorry for themselves. They can of course heal if they could look at the shadow side of themselves, but unfortunately they are in such denial of this part they can't see it, nor do they appear to care to look too deeply at this time. They often feel like the victim and often feel not good enough.

Rheumatoid arthritis is tied into having much fear of what the future holds for them. The more that these individuals work on cultivating faith, the more they would try not to compete with anyone else, but rather learn to look deep within the power of their own minds. These are ones with great wisdom buried so deeply that it becomes impossible for them to look within. They are freezing in fear about many things that are happening in their life simultaneously, and if they don't have much to worry about they will find something or someone such as family members or friends to focus their energy on, rather than themselves and their own creativity that they no longer wish to use. They often become disgusted with their condition and do not wish to go forward in any area of their life, which of course makes it even more difficult for them with symptoms and the progression of the disease. As with anyone, they will become stuck physically and/or emotionally if they do not go forward into the light of the higher self. There are many individuals and places where these people can receive assistance. Often, however, they have a false sense of pride that lies behind their insecurities of a personal nature.

What one with rheumatoid arthritis can do is look at themselves directly in the eye and learn how to laugh at themselves, which is something very hard for them to do; to realize that this is something they themselves have conjured up in order to learn to laugh and be free. They are often so full of fear that the condition progresses. The best thing for them to do is to try new things. No matter what they do, just changing their routine can and will work wonders for them. The body needs to know that it can move in many different directions, but it often gets stuck in certain positions and freezes in fear of the unknown.

These individuals are often frightened of what others think of them. They are more interested in being like everyone else and also being quiet. They are so insecure they often will not show their true feelings, mostly because they do not even know how they feel. To get to the ego is not something they want to look at and deal with, so they distract themselves with the symptoms and distractions of their illness. This is one that causes them to bring attention to themselves, but in some way this is exactly what they do not want on the level of the ego. The spirit, however, does want and needs the positive attention it deserves. These individuals have so much to say; however, somewhere along the line they were told they were unintelligent or stupid and what they had to offer would not help anyone anywhere or anyway. They stopped trying to help and offer advice because they are so afraid of rejection. They stopped reaching out and calling some because they have this feeling now of entitlement so that others will come to them because they feel guilty (as they should, according to them.) There is much envy in these individuals at this time in their life. They are learning how to be humble and how to ask for help in a way they have never had to do. Financially, they often have trouble and blame it on their condition. Of course the condition caused by their spirit has manifested in order to encourage them to try new things and let a lot of the old things go. Those with rheumatoid often hoard things because they are afraid they might need something, anything, and this is because they feel they are not getting anything or enough from anyone else. They need to keep holding on to the old in the area of emotions, things, people, jobs, etc., because they do not wish to go forward in any area of their life, especially aging. They might want to meditate on the old profound saying of "being as old as you feel" and perhaps work on that idea.

Many of those with rheumatoid feel lonely and melancholy and again experience much fear. Now what one must do to feel better and perhaps heal is, first of all, to let go of any sarcastic nature they may have. They are often looking to see if someone is trying to "rip them off". They do not trust easily and at times they do not make the best parents or partners because they are too self-absorbed. This is, however, a secret self-absorption.

It often seems there is a lot of negativity in this person's personality. However, the truth is that the light of God is so strong in them that the darkness must seem so large. This condition is about keeping up with the passions of one's spirit. These souls live their life for others and often forget about themselves on a soul level. They want so much to see everyone else have a good time that they don't often think of how they themselves could have fun. They would also allow others to do everything for them if possible, as a way for them to receive what they feel they truly deserve. They also, at important times, have a hard time expressing decency and love. Another issue to be looked at is that they are not the best cheerleaders for others or themselves. They must learn to encourage themselves first and then they can step up to the plate for others, but not before. As the condition progresses they become more and more like their own parents, and the symptoms of that alone can potentially become very irritating to themselves, as well as those they love.

If those with rheumatoid are given even a small amount of love they rapidly respond. Once again, they are often love-starved, but what they must understand is that they must learn to love and care for themselves first. It is crucial that they spend more time and energy loving and caring for themselves. They do not need to develop an illness in order to justify pleasing themselves. Lastly, there is generally so much boredom and a sense of giving up and hopelessness that it can be a very difficult illness to overcome. But, just as any condition or ailment it is created so that a soul can heal itself and open, grow, and mature spiritually. It is very important that these individuals learn to see themselves most especially with the eyes of the Divine and when they can really do this their entire lives will certainly turn around and the inspirations that they will acquire will be plentiful. Rheumatoid is so much about encouragement and the lack of it in one's life. Learning to encourage others as well as themselves is key when someone finds themselves in this predicament. Their heart in some places has turned into stone which is common and actually quite natural for all human beings who have been wounded by others' insecurity and mediocrity. All human beings must go through this process, but those with this particular condition would benefit greatly from quickly and quietly expressing immediate and constant encouragement towards themselves and others as well as really increasing their faith and the theology skills that lies dormant in many of these souls. They tend to be intuitive and very advanced often times and these spiritual gifts want desperately to be recognized and reborn fully as they enter into the next part of their lives without pain and internal torture that manifests itself in the physical body as well as the mental and emotional bodies. Those with rheumatoid arthritis can potentially evolve into excellent healers and teachers of Spirit because they have often lived the darkest of times. ⚹

SCIATICA

Making a Concrete Plan in order to Achieve
the Best and Most Out of Life
Learning How to Open Up Honestly More to Self and Others

Sciatica comes from a part of the brain that is extremely judgmental about a part of themselves. It's a part that the individual who suffers from this condition finds intolerable, and very often is kept in deep disguise because they are so ashamed of their deepest feelings of grief. Sciatica is a nerve irritation that mirrors the interior irritation of one's own self. These individuals often feel that they should be doing something other than what their heart is really wanting to sing about, yet sometimes screams to do so in the form of sciatica. The sciatica forces one to slow down. When it acts up it is actually an outburst of the little one inside that carries on in extreme and often painful ways so that she or he may have a chance at last of really being heard. Sciatica is often the call of making a concrete plan of one's life for the present and near future. What this particular pain is calling for is healing of the psyche in a rather large and distinct way. There are a few and sometimes many changes in one's life that are being asked for. Some attention in the manner of life after death and the organization of one's life is needed. This condition is about making the best and most of life. Often these individuals have many unused talents, which are unused out of fear and the worry of things that are most likely never going to happen.

Individuals who experience sciatica often go to extremes to hide from others in the way of thinking that they are protecting themselves, but what they are really doing is "hiding out" so that their real feelings are not disclosed for fear of abandonment. When one is in a flare-up of sciatica, they must look within and ask themselves, *What am I most afraid of in this moment? What am I not willing to acknowledge within myself that I am often perhaps too frequently about to notice in another?*

Lasting relief will come to these sufferers if they are really willing to look at their own shadow and truly pray about and seek to find ways to reveal and heal that shadow. If this is done, or at least a conscious effort is made, one will not need to be in such pain. There are many past fears clogged in the body and when there is an attack of sciatica one is really saying to oneself in body language that you are ready to do some deep inner work. If you say and really mean that you are ready, then a teacher, an insight, a healer, etc. will appear to aid you in more of the discovery of yourself.

The breath and following it all day long will also help tremendously. Ask yourself what will make you happy and pleasant in this moment. Often sciatica is a way to motivate you to find ways to pleasure yourself, which you do not often look to do. Many times the sufferer of this condition feels that they have no time to have a good time. They are tremendously busy and tend to feel very put upon by others, so that when they have an attack of sciatica they feel justified in saying no to others and getting the down time that they need. However, the down time they need is playtime and relaxation time and should not be about painful forced down time. Also it has nothing to do with being put upon by others. Sciatica has to do with not giving yourself enough quality time. If one has regular playtime scheduled into their life they will need less and less sciatica symptoms.

Sciatica sufferers sometimes feel like a "Little Miss No Name," which means that they have forgotten how real and alive within their inner child is and also how powerful she or he is. Sciatica is a great reminder that no matter how old one gets one must discover the gold within their own souls and remember that there is a plan. A very divine plan that the gold is distributed and discovered over one's lifetime and one can never stop mining for it for very long. It is strongly suggested that when sciatica comes banging on your door you answer it and very seriously start making a plan and some promises to yourself to have fun and know that in that fun and relaxation is most often how the new gold will be discovered. It is in discovering this gold that one discovers more and more of the Godself and therefore will need less and less symptoms and screams of the soul trying to be set free. The happy playful one within must be heard.

These individuals tend to have a unique grace to their personalities that when happy, content, and well fed emotionally, physically, and intellectually, are some of the most wonderfully loving and giving individuals on the planet. If they do not take care of themselves in these ways they can be most stubborn, unhealthy, and unhappy. It is crucial, therefore, for these individuals to learn how to open up honestly more to themselves and others. This is a very important part of their spiritual, psychological, and physical growth and healing. This can be difficult for them because they are often quite sensitive and do not show their sensitivities but to a select few where they feel safe to expose the more vulnerable parts of themselves.

Sciatica is very much about healing the mind, body, and soul. It is really about opening to all ways of healing. Sciatica sufferers are often healing individuals and with the learning of various forms of healing for themselves, especially deep relaxation techniques, they will find great joy in teaching these techniques to others as well. ☘

SCOLIOSIS KYPHOSIS

Opportunity to Release Energy from the Higher Self
in order to Allow Discovery of Passions
Learning to Go Within to Find One's Own Answers

This form of curvature of the spine comes when one is very stubborn in the way of helping others to see the truth without their own fears being in the way. These individuals are very intellectual to the point of self-sabotaging their own incredible intuitive nature. They are insecure in how they can easily give away their power to someone they think is an authority figure. The truth, however, is that it is they who are their own best authority. They simply must work as hard on relaxing their body and mind as they do working it to get more information. Usually, these individuals do not stop for very long looking for some form of help from other sources, but the *Source* that they least pursue is the one of the Most High and it is the one that they can locate all on their own. What lodges in the spine is the neglect of the soul and it distorts just like the mind and spirit.

Scoliosis kyphosis is a form of discontent that lodges in the spine. The energy from the higher self is lodged in there and it must be released in order to relieve the symptoms. The form may not change, but the pain can greatly ease, and even completely release, if one is bold enough and desperate enough to surrender into one's own passions. Mostly, however, these individuals do not know what their passions are and that void also is lodged energetically in the spine. One must really get to the core of their innermost being, and see just what it is that they would like to do for the rest of their lives. These individuals must do an evaluation of sorts.

By doing an evaluation, what is meant is that these individuals are being asked to cultivate as much information in the area of self-pleasure as they can. This is the most important information for them to gather, and absorb, and put to good use. Often, this is the last bit of information they think to gather. They are often barking up the wrong tree, so to speak, in what needs the most attention in their lives. What is being asked of these individuals is that they get to know quite well who they are, who they really are on the deepest levels.

Somewhere in time when these individuals were growing up they felt very lost and frightened about life and the meaning of it. There was confusion of which way to go and who to go to for the truth. They did not often trust one or both of their parents because they sensed such confusion in them that they were afraid to go to them with their questions for fear of becoming even more confused. These individuals grow, then, with many unanswered questions, and a fear of going within for their own answers. What is most important is that they come to terms with the way they were raised with the lack of concern for their well-being, which of course was not intentional but something quite distorting to this one's psyche. This is what is lodged in the spine and will be released as one learns to listen to the Divine within them. There is much wasted time looking outside of themselves and not enough looking within. This is worth repeating, as this is the most important piece of their puzzle.

The body often distorts when the mind is very confused in the area of substance and essential spiritual progress. These individuals have been stunted somewhere in time and it is up to them to discover the lost pieces of their soul that hides in the spine, lodging itself along the interior walls of the spine, traveling all the way into the genitals and bowels of the person with this condition.

What must be done is to learn to go to the deepest part of themselves, including the most personal and intimate parts of their lives and become very acquainted with these aspects of themselves, including the most basic and the most pure without shame or fear. One must learn, or rather relearn, the basics of life and teach themselves as if they were teaching their own child with all the care and concern that was not given to them for whatever reason when they were young. The reason(s) do not matter. All that matters is the absence of the care and concern they needed. The truth is that all that care and concern is alive and well beneath their own spine and no one but them can give to themselves and love themselves the way only they can do. This is the crucial piece of healing. Everything they do not understand in life or are not at peace with must be written down over time and dealt with, little by little, with great care and concern. This information must be meditated on and marinated in and little by little the spine will release the pieces of the soul lost long ago. Many lifetimes can be lodged inside of a person's spine waiting until this one is to be recognized and released by the one who walks with it.

There are many gifts in disguise waiting to be recognized and released. These individuals are learning how to have a good time in the simplest of situations and how to speak out their truth without fear of rejection from those they love or want to love. Scoliosis kyphosis is of great importance to the one who carries it for the growth of their spirit and the freedom of their soul. Their creativity, as well as the Source of their creativity lives and breathes within their spine and the way to release it is to look at it as healthy, wealthy, and wise at all times, because it is absolutely full of wisdom and the power to create. The artist within must look to demonstrate these qualities each and every day and often in the most difficult of circumstances. This is the greatest challenge of those with this condition. One must remember all is possible with the arms, heart, eyes, and the mind of Love.

SEIZURES

Allowing the Vulnerability and Soul Exposure Necessary
for the Achievement of One's Destiny
Opportunity for Surrendering Into One's Most
Pure and Developed Form

The truth of what is occurring when one has a seizure is that the potential to be a more honest and clearly spoken individual is present more than ever before. The seizure alters one's brain so that they could live on the Earth plane with more comfort and ease. Although this one lives much of the time with their head and heart wanting very much to be in the clouds with the Divine, their life and its structure, and the part of them that still has their heart unconsciously located in the brain, causes them to suffer tremendous heartache. Eventually, a seizure comes to let this soul release the part of them that is afraid of being exposed for the *lover* and the *lover of God* that they really have in storage of their cells. The seizure adds necessary release and relief as this soul has had a hard time letting go.

This person often stands in judgment of other human beings. When he or she comes in contact with another who speaks the word and does the work of God they remember a part of their own soul who wants only to do this work as well, but they still have work of their own ego left to do. The ego has served as necessary protection for them in the past and needs to be recognized and blessed as doing so in order for this one to let go and move further in the direction of the higher Divine self. When a seizure or the fear of having one occurs, it is telling this soul that it is time to lose control and dance with *the wild ones*, those who are hopelessly in love with the Divine and its mind. Others who come in contact with this person desperately need to see into this soul more deeply because they too are working their way to the wild ones and the *side* of the ones who live with their heads in the Breast of the Divine.

There is great sadness in these individuals that comes from many lifetimes of working very deeply with others, yet seeing still so much suffering and separation of the Divine that they could not aid. In this lifetime, however, they certainly can help others in this way, but they must first expose the part of themselves that stands in judgment of not a one. This soul is ready to spread their wings to the greatest of spans, yet they still cannot release and let go out of the fear of being an exposed soul for all to see. There was an important point in their life where they got stuck. He or she was such a sensitive child and somehow they were humiliated beyond control of hiding their humiliation. They cried and cried, but tried to hide, and because they could not, they stood still in that time and it stuck deep inside of their brain and moved on into their heart. At that time they put an energetic lock on their heart and said something like this, *There will never again come a time that I do this again, so I can and will humiliate another to make myself feel better.* Of course, this only makes it worse. This individual is not aware of what he or she does to others and their psyches when they speak and reprimand. In doing such they make others afraid to speak their truth for fear they will humiliate them as well. This of course keeps the true soul in seclusion when it comes to deeper connection with others and this connection is deeply craved. It also prevents one from their own solid connection with themselves and God.

Seizures come to those who are of the highest accord and to those who have suffered greatly as masters in past lives in that they laid down their own life for those that they loved. In this life this person never feels quite loved enough or loved in the *right* way and so secretly or unconsciously will judge many of those they love and become, generally, a person of judgment. This soul commands the attention of just about anyone on their path, which is rightfully deserved as they most often bring to the earth much needed information and healing. They can also, however, bring much discouragement as well because those around them often feel they could never catch up to them, nor feel they have much to offer them. This brings sadness and loneliness to the one who suffers with this condition more than anything else during the midlife years.

Along with each seizure much of the ego is discharged and one remembers more of the caliber of the divinity, which they carry a little too tightly and privately within their own soul. This person wants so desperately to be free to love without conditions that he or she will create seizures, or even just the fear of having one, so that they can then let go in ways they cannot on their own. The reason being is that this part of their natural divine nature has yet to be fully exposed or accepted and must be in order to achieve their highest calling and fulfill their destiny. In fact, this individual does not feel worthy of or in connection to the Divine on a regular basis, and when they are in the company of where they are free to access and expose this they can close down even further. This is when the potential for a seizure is even greater.

One way to aid in self-healing is by going as often as possible into Divine waters. Bathe alone in a quiet space, create a salt bath ritual, or travel to sacred places that allow and encourage bathing. Allow the bath to extricate the toxins that are energetically picked up after having been around many people. The reason they are picking up toxins rather than letting them pass through them is that they are still in such deep hiding of who they really are. The truth with this soul is that they are one who can devour an entire town with their love and can also destroy it as well with the hesitancy of acceptance of their divine nature. It is crucial that this soul accepts the beauty, love, wisdom, and spiritual courage that they have hiding deep within just waiting for all to see and utilize in healing themselves as well. Seizures represent the part of the brain that lives in seclusion of one's own personality as well as others. This person will not allow themselves to be vulnerable; however, seizures and the fear of having them actually create the vulnerability necessary to become who one has been put on the earth to become.

This person is often one with great teaching ability, aiding individuals in learning important lessons extremely quickly, but also is not one to force feed anyone, and can become quite annoyed if and when someone does not understand his or her concepts, or their way of life. There is a time coming soon, however, that this person will completely surrender their way to inner peace and finally come to terms with the part of themselves that is divine beyond comprehension. This person tends to worry about where others see him or her in light of their own divinity, yet they themselves do not yet accept this; therefore, others cannot as well. They often then can become the target for much judgment and disapproval. This individual is attracting much of what he or she puts out in the way of his or her own frustration and inner turmoil and hell. They are the sole creator of all. This is partially because they show their true love to only a few, compared to the many that they can. They are working on knowing and becoming completely free to be the consummate human being they came to be, as well as to show the world. There is much information stored within the seizure itself, as well as the threat of one. This person does not know how to rid themselves of the fear of being exposed, but the more they expose their truest and most holy self, the faster they will not need the threat or actual presentation of the seizures.

The actual event of a seizure may also occur when one is sleeping and not conscious as to what is happening. Seizures often go unrecognized, but what is happening during a seizure is a direct visit and communication from the Divine in which much love is deeply injected to speed up the process of this soul who has come first and most importantly to touch and create the love of the Lord wherever they go. It is their own soul who shall not be satisfied and completely happy until they surrender to their purest and most developed form, and it is the soul who always finds its way to victory no matter how long it may take.

SINUSITIS

Opportunity for the Fulfillment of Desire for the Exposure of One's Soul
Learning to Release Deep Feelings and Connect with the God Within

Sinusitis comes from the place of one's heart where he lingers, but no longer remains or belongs. Chronic issues are stored in the tissues where the release of tears are stored for far too long. This individual needs deep release and cleansing of grief held onto from long ago. There is a time that this person holds onto for the sake of the rest of the family. He often feels he must hold it together, but his togetherness is in the form of illusion and he has not tackled the part of his soul that has been holding on to very uncomfortable circumstances without feeling his real feelings. The body will always not only cry the tears a person will refuse to, but will also develop the absolute best situations and or condition(s) so that one can release all of their tensions. Sinusitis affects people who are highly stressed and cannot release their stress very well, and often they do not even attempt to release it. Instead they tend to carry it in their heads and sinus areas. Surrounding tissues and muscles can then become very arrested and energy is blocked and the tissues become irritated and inflamed.

Sinusitis comes from living in the head and not enough in the heart – so much so that one gets depleted without much reason. Much rest is needed and, often, this is not appreciated by others and they themselves think they must not rest for too long, as they may not get up again. The truth is they would like to hold in their feelings forever, but this is not going to happen because the soul desires great exposure and connection with the Divine, as well as all of Spirit Life. This soul does not take nearly enough time for relaxing with the Divine alone and on his own. He can take time with friends and family, but what he needs most is time alone so that he can feel the depths of his own soul, not that so much of others, which is often the case. This soul tends to get caught up in the emotions of others as well as their troubles and worries. He then has no space or time to process his own, as he will not even be aware of his feelings – most importantly, his dissatisfaction in life. He spends much time looking for the cure or fantasizing and worrying about feeling good.

This individual tends to feel desperate and alone even though there are many who love him. This person does not often put himself at the top of the list. He must come to terms with who he is and what he is feeling. He is afraid of becoming like someone in his family or in his imagination. By this, what is meant is that a part of him feels unsuccessful in love or career. The body is creating and feeling the pain that he refuses to feel so that he can make some changes in his life. There is often not much true support in his life by others. This one looks for approval from others who simply cannot support themselves enough, so there is no way they could give this soul what he is looking for. Now the truth is that this one must learn to go to the top – right to the top – and that means to go to God. There is not much support in the physical world because this soul tends to not feel as good as many of those around him. There is a problem or concern most often of truly relating on a soul level with those he loves. He cannot seem to truly express himself. Those who do support him most often have a very hard time letting him fend for himself, which is most of what he desires on a soul level so that he can grow and expand spiritually and psychologically. There is a well of sadness that must be expired in this soul so that he can heal the wounds of the past. He is often a martyr on a level of introspection.

He must not go to the past, but only to the moment and to the *now* time. This is what will heal and aid him in progression and release of his tensions.

This soul is often preoccupied with his symptoms of body so that he does not have to feel his feelings. This is not a conscious choice; however, this is something that he must look more deeply into without being hard on himself. This one has negative feelings stored away about someone or others who are close to him and is tormented by guilt about his feelings. They are often so suppressed that they are felt in the body, especially the head and the mind and the upper part of the shoulders and neck. This is the section of the body that is most connected to one's psychic and spiritual world and this is what desires to be explored. The *mystic within* this soul is not about to give up his place in the world of Spirit, which is the *real world*, so he suffers until he really makes a breakthrough for himself, as well as the world. He is much needed in the way of service to humankind and God's dream. If he would only give permission to himself to do what pleases him most and make the time for those pleasures, well then, his world as well as his body, mind and spirit shall heal as his soul opens and evolves.

SOCIOPATH

A Tremendous Opportunity for the Light to Be Born Indirectly
Representation of the Shadow Side of the World
Opportunity for Learning The Highest Form of Love
Can Be Not Being Available

A sociopath is one who has the God within them living so vaguely they cannot truly connect to anyone no matter how closely related or in love they may pretend to be. This individual does not know what their deepest feelings are and live in a land within their own mind, as if on an island where there are no people, not even themselves most of the time. They have no rules and live with no regrets, having very little in the way of mainstream or collective thinking. Sociopaths get confused in that they tend to regard themselves in many areas of their life as if they were a king or queen and live regally within their own mind. As such, if they are not treated royally, entitled to receiving whatever they desire, there is a need to emotionally hurt, injure, and/or victimize others, often in strange, very uncomfortable and awkward ways. In extreme cases a sociopath can even kill. Something triggers within and their instinct becomes to harm those they love, live with, or are in association with in some way.

These individuals often believe that they have been put on the earth to create a better world; however, the fashion in which they act is often times perceived as bizarre by others. What actually ends up being created is confusion and sadness for those around them, as well as for their own souls, which are already deeply wounded, although they generally have no idea that they are, in fact, in need of healing. Furthermore, the sociopathic person strongly desires to remove anyone from their mind who has the ability to see their shadow side. This very difficult condition is one where, often times, others wish to get away from this person not knowing exactly why, as a sociopath is often in a brilliant masquerade.

A sociopath is one who is lost in the tunnel where heaven and earth meet in the middle, which means that spiritually, they are neither here nor there and look to wander into the minds and hearts of others, as if to feed off their lifeline, rather than create and generate their own spiritual development and soul's evolution. This is a very sad condition and one that is hard to understand, rationalize, and as well, to forgive in these people. A person like this has been incarnated to see the world through the eyes of the Divine, but cannot remove the blinders worn over their hearts and minds. They retreat into their own mind and thoughts when things get difficult for them, which is often, especially as they grow older with time on this side.

A sociopath holds the position of the insanity of the world and serves as the mirror of that insanity. They cannot see or feel the oneness of all people because they do not consider themselves part of anything such as, and especially, in a position of spiritual truth. The worlds in which those who have this condition vary drastically. This is such a deep disguise and those who carry this gene of *man-made* wear a mask so thick and frightening at times that others run from them when they begin to see the truth of the falsehood in which this person lives. The sociopathic person is living a lie most of the time. They can be with others acting and/or appearing to be polite, charming, and literally, as if they bring the sun wherever they go. This, however, is the most dangerous type of sociopath as neither they nor anyone else can live masquerading as the light for too long a time, as this is when fire is caught on and they become ragingly angry at those who are supposed to be their friends and those seemingly loved and kept close to the heart. It is important for those in close relationship with this individual to know that this person's heart is one where there is so much trouble and confusion that they are incapable of and have very little desire (consciously or unconsciously) for opening and healing themselves. The person with this condition also cares very little for the highest good of others.

The higher purpose of a sociopath is to illuminate the ones who have brought them to this point. An important spiritual lesson that must be learned is to never look at anyone as a god/goddess-type or lover before one learns to truly love themselves. There is a shadow side to every human being and the sociopath, similar to a terrorist, represents for everyone the shadow of the world. This shadow lives in everyone to varying degrees and during this time of evolution there is divine purpose for this condition, as well as the existence of terrorism and both will remain until the world is brought to its knees as one in the light of love and the divine nature of the human and its heart.

The condition of sociopath shall continue until humankind can truly see themselves in every one of God's creatures and that includes every human being. In order for a sociopath to heal, those around him or her must ask many questions and investigate their answers and never be afraid to ask the advice of others in this case because so much fear is generated by the sociopathic personality and the natural tendency is for them to seek out those who are unconditionally loving to the point where their kindness is often taken advantage of. Those involved with them always want to give another chance, and while this response is most holy it can perpetuate the condition. Sometimes the highest form of love is to not be available. People become quite addicted to their crime and punishment, which is mirrored within one's conditions. This is no different, but because of the degree of shadow involved there is tremendous opportunity for the light to be born indirectly. This means every person is always playing their role working for the light in their own way. This condition shall be eradicated when enlightenment is much more common than not. ⸙

STROKE

A Time to Shine in One's Divine Light and Discover True Purpose
Learning to Bless Situations for Spiritual Healing
to Take Root and Grow

When someone has a stroke what has occurred metaphysically is that one's heart is in a major process of redirecting itself. The highest purpose of one's life is being asked to be taken on at this time. After some recuperation, this person is in need of asking themselves questions concerning the deeper meaning of their life. Questions such as, *Why are they here? Why do they feel and think that they had the stroke? What do they want to do with the rest of their lives?*

Spiritually and metaphysically speaking, there are no victims. However, individuals who have had a stroke often feel as though they are a victim of circumstance. They tend to not take much action, and sometimes no action at all, in the way of making their lives easier for themselves. They are often caretakers of others in an emotional sense and sometimes physical as well. They are ones to offer assistance and then wonder why they said they would do something. Those who have suffered a stroke need to get things in a big way in order to make the necessary shifts in their lives that will facilitate the changes that will serve themselves, as well as others.

The stroke is a metaphysical or nonphysical way of getting someone to reorganize their life and the people in it. It is also a way that one is forced – actually – into being more real and more mindful of their own time, and not be so willing to give it away any longer. This is something they have been avoiding to do, but they must learn to practice what they preach to others so freely. These individuals are often very good at counseling others to make their lives run more efficiently; however, when it comes to their own life, they give much too much of themselves away. They tend to sell their souls, so to speak, and then can become quite resentful, but in a very hidden way. Often, the stroke is a way to get out one's deepest feelings without having to talk about them with anyone. This person does not like confrontation and will avoid it at all cost, except when it is with someone they know unconditionally loves them and they can feel sure they will still be loved, wanted, and needed.

A stroke occurs when one is much too bored with life on a daily basis. These individuals need some attention for themselves, as they are pretty tired of giving to others what they must finally learn to give to themselves. The stroke is a glorious but painful way on many levels of mind, body, and soul to get one to grow and find their true purpose in this lifetime. They will often go to great lengths in order to not do or have their heart's desire. This is a very sad situation for them. They often take regular jobs that are more reliable and stable, but less exciting and challenging than they are actually capable of. These individuals tend to make wonderful teachers and programmers of computers, etc. However, they often prefer to stay in situations where they are not the center of attention. The stroke and its condition forces them to be in the center and have much-needed concern about them be in the making. The stroke also leads one to his destination in the way of finance planning and relationship problem solving. It is a time of reevaluation for these individuals. Unless they want more struggle and heartache they need to surrender to all the positivity that wants to emerge from their often-temporary condition.

An interesting thing about having a stroke is that its occurrence and reality in this person's mind makes for a great loss of fear of rejection, which tends to be an issue with those who have had a stroke. Many fears in one's life can be eliminated after a stroke, but it usually takes its time in leaving the human system because the stroke itself carries so many burdens and new problems that force the one suffering to really take care of themselves and, most importantly, be the one who needs the caring for. It is actually a great opportunity to learn over again many things that one can learn better now than the first time around. One really begins to use his imagination, which is where reality begins, and one can start then to stand out in a crowd where this was often a problem before the stroke. Having a stroke is something that brings up many problems and concerns that must be brought to the surface so one can clear them up and move on. If the stroke did not occur this person could have ended up living a very boring and underutilized life. One must bless their condition over and over again in order for the spiritual healing to take root and grow. And, as it does, so does the human psyche, which has manifested the condition so one can ultimately become a very productive and satisfied human being, having much to offer humankind.

These individuals tend to be the leaders in their own families. The stroke offers a way for them to now let others be the leaders, which allows this one to rest and take a backseat to everyone else's life, so he can just focus on his own life and tend to a secret wish: to give himself the chance to shine. A stroke can actually force one's light to shine, although it can take a while, which can be just fine because, like a fine wine, when one heals slowly but surely, he becomes delicious and his sense of humor becomes a real healing tool for himself and others. A real playful spirit wants to emerge, and if he is encouraged, so shall that be. He will then be one that everyone feels well and happy around more than ever before.

Once the initial shock of the stroke is over, one can get on and use the situation for all it has to offer in the way of becoming an enlightened soul. And, if one has the intention to use his condition for all it is worth, and surrender into having the stroke and all that comes with it, one will grow beyond their wildest dreams. They will become so incredibly supportive to other human beings and, most importantly, they will first become supportive to themselves.

Lastly, the stroke offers one many opportunities to tie up loose ends, especially in the area of relationships. For example, they may marry the person of their dreams. All the concepts of marriage or partnership on any level that has been important to the individual can now be realized. The stroke advises one to learn to be a partner to themselves first and foremost, as one can only then be a partner to another in every sense of the word. Very important also, this condition encourages one to dissolve any ties that no longer serve their soul and the highest purpose and vision of themselves. The true self is free to now be reborn and stand more firmly – always – in the light of the higher self.

TOOTHACHES & MOUTH PROBLEMS

A Time to Create Newness In One's Life
A Container for One's Dreams and the Birth of Their Reality

The teeth come into play when one must be very careful of how he or she is speaking to others in their life that they have much love for, yet are concerned with their actions. This person with a toothache has problems and irritation with those who are of stubborn nature, and also those who are not classical in their training. If one is suffering from tooth problems of any sort it is time that this individual changes courses in their life, as well as in their diet. They are being asked by the higher self to either drink less wine, or eat less sugar, and to eat more healthily in general. Fish is a very important part of their nutrition and its value at the time of a toothache.

The teeth and their problems metaphysically mean that they have been feeling incredibly stifled lately in their lives, and things are finally starting to move. The toothache is the *martyr within* coming to take away some of their newfound joy and friends. When one has a toothache one must look within and ask themselves some questions. How honest are they being with others, but more importantly, how honest are they being with themselves? This person has high amounts of passion, yet he is stifled in letting those passions out more regularly. He is often one of high intelligence, but one who suffers when he is in the company of someone not on his level of importance and circumstance.

The toothache often happens at a time in his life when all is okay, but not very exciting. Well, not exciting enough for this soul in this particular moment, as this one can take on a huge amount of lights, camera, and action, so to speak. He is ready to conquer the world and the fear or resistance comes within the tooth to keep him a bit contained for a little while so he does not spill his seed too soon. He is waiting for the soil to be ready to plant the trees he is envisioning to grow. This soul, when he is annoyed by a tooth problem, is being shown where someone, and it is most often a someone but can be a situation as well, is really annoying them with their lack of action or commitment. This one is easily frustrated by those who are less conscious than himself and the toothache is about those learning patience for his fellow human beings. This one is often many miles ahead of those around him. There is intense sadness held within him and it must come out in some way. The tooth is where he chews in the mouth in which he must swallow many things that bring him pain and frustration.

What the teeth and the mouth metaphysically mean with their problems is about the learning to let go of the things one no longer needs, especially in the way of money, fame, or fortune, and to be free enough to just be and give himself the time to relax in the grace of God and the grace of others. When a tooth aches it is the time to be in relation or connection with family and friends of a very simple life. The tooth is crying for the world, as well as missing the world once known to this person who is suffering. The pain that is unacknowledged is trying to release and trying to be acknowledged, which it must be or something else will crop up and cause disorder of something else. This one is in need of emotional release. A cry during the time of a toothache is often very encouraging and then something of great mouthwatering acknowledgment of a piece of the Divine – something new, never felt before is coming through – but this one is wanting to give away something that is just for him. This cannot occur as the higher self within is stopping this dark action of the ego. So the passion and the gift that is suppressed within is being felt rather than a gift as an ache of the tooth.

This tooth most likely needs attention from a dentist and may be finished in this life and have to be replaced or filled or crowned or whatever a dentist can do. But if and when the work is done so will the emotional piece and the gift will come out as well. The ache of a tooth often also means one is longing to be touched in and on the physical body. The soul sometimes creates pain in the area of the mouth or the teeth as this one needs tender loving care. A massage can be of great service by the self or another as soon as a tooth begins to hurt. To read or to be read to, especially beautiful literature, is very much in need. It is a piece of the child that just wants to play and stop the rush of work. There is no race to be won. You already wear the crown that you are searching for.

When a tooth aches it also means it is time to create a new life, turn over a new leaf. Fear not what the Spirit of the Lord has in store for you because it is going to be of much fun and creativity and it is on its way to you in ways you have never dreamed. The teeth represent the part of the self that needs to move, to wiggle and shake and play. Rolling on a ball can also relieve the pain, as well as medication if needed. Peppermint often will work wonders, too.

There is a dream planted in each tooth and as those dreams are realized a tooth will feel the birth of that dream and that is not usually painless unless, of course, the tooth simply breaks. Whatever the physical cause may be, which can be age, weakness, or injury, metaphysically speaking, it is just the opposite. It is a container. The mouth and teeth are a container for our dreams and the birth of their reality.

There is also the way of the mouth and the teeth that we must look at ourselves in a very honest way, more honest than ever, about what we want and where we want to be and where we see ourselves in the moment, as well as the future. The issues with the mouth are about dreaming big and letting go of the dreams that no longer serve our highest good. And, most importantly, it is about our expression of those dreams to others as well as ourselves.

AFTERWORD

"A little metaphysical knowledge goes a very long way."

It is not always easy to live in a metaphysical world, but I have often found that a little metaphysical knowledge goes a very long way. It is my hope, prayer, and with deepest sincerity that I wish for these words to travel around the globe, reaching as many people as possible, for I have achieved astonishing essential progress while being a universal force of dedicated spiritual healing made wonderfully possible and available by the advancement of social media. The daily utilization of vehicles such as Facebook pages, The MetaPhysician Within blog site, Twitter accounts, etc., have radically confirmed that love and healing are generated spirit to spirit. It is nothing short of miraculous that one can be anywhere in the world and with just a click, touch another soul in deep and profound ways. I have been blessed numerous times by being a part of such encounters. So, although this manual has been just about ready for some time, what I know for sure is that there is something very important -- as important as our conditions of mind and body -- and that is the essentiality of Divine Timing, for the spiritual community reached and cultivated during these past few years has given me an international forum of Divine Recognition and ability to serve and be served by offering my gifts freely. So far social media for me has proven to be a realistic mystic's dream come true -- for one can be alone in their studio creating in the ways of writing, photographing, painting, etc., while simultaneously and truly one with the entire world. As with every new technology comes fear, doubts, and surprises, as well as in this case a great deal of love, healing, and inspired thinking. The positive has far outweighed the negative and continues to show more gains each day as people learn how to love and be one in the age of social media.

A NOTE FROM LISA

I wish to thank you for reading and working with this manual of healing. I bless the work and the life it took to complete it. The chapters have gone through me like a river of love as I opened myself up to the Divine Intelligence and was used --just as everyone can be utilized -- by the Divine to bring the light to the darkest corners of the human mind, body, and spirit.

With this offering, I give to you my light, love, and all good things.

In Divine Love and Guidance may you live the life of your dreams as you live life to your fullest.

Lisa

ACKNOWLEDGEMENTS

I acknowledge fully the Divine Intelligence, the Beloved within myself, and all else. As well, I bless the shadow within all because it certainly is serving a crucial role in the healing of the Earth and the Spirit of its people. It is in the acceptance and sincere blessing of the darkness that the light is shown. All events are holy and all events lead us closer to true, pure Divine love…to our Godself…to the sublime. May you be as blessed in reading and utilizing this body of work as I was in writing it.

To my family, Rob, R.J., Philip, and Christian, you are the greatest lights in my life and certainly have been an important part of the creation and manifestation of The MetaPhysician Within. I love you deeply, adore you each entirely, and cherish you tremendously.

Lisa

ABOUT THE PHOTOGRAPHIC IMAGES

Included in The MetaPhysician Within are some of my photographic images from The Divine Garden collection. I find black and white images, especially, to offer a wonderfully deep contemplative intensity. I also find them to be incredibly stimulating while capturing the timeless beauty and deep mysticism of Nature. I adore working in this way. I find it passionate, intriguing and alluring, as well as an absolute joy keeping me in a mesmerized state each time I work with Nature's jewels. To be able to bring as much as I possibly can to reveal their truest nature and power to transform the mind, body and spirit is my greatest honor, blessing, and joy.

Blessings and Namaste,

Lisa

ABOUT LISA A. BLACKMAN

Lisa A. Blackman is the author of *The Metaphysician Within* and an internationally known intuitive healer and spiritual teacher who helps people to open and rapidly evolve their souls aiding them in self-discovery, healing and transformation of mind, body and spirit. She is also a poet and the author of *Spirit Life: Ecstatic Poetry and Prayers* and an artist whose photographic images often illustrate her writing. Lisa has 20 years experience in the field of spiritual health and healing and maintains a private practice, learning center and studio on the East Coast where she lectures, exhibits her art and lives with her family in Connecticut.

You can learn more about Lisa and her work by visiting
www.lisablackman.org.

www.lisablackman.org

Lisa A. Blackman Publishing

Fairfield, CT 06824

(203) 254-8416